SQUAD CARS

THE DURBAN POLICE DOG UNIT IN THE 1970S

SID BRETTELL

squadcarsdbn@gmail.com

Interior and cover crafted with love by the team at www.myebook.online

Squad Cars: The Durban Police Dog Unit in the 1970s

– First Edition.

ISBN 978-1-5272-4386-6

CONTENTS

FOREWORD

South Africa in the 1960s and 70s was a country subjected to sanctions and boycotts by the international community because of its fundamentally flawed apartheid policy with its system of segregation and discrimination on the grounds of race.

The South African Police Dog Unit started in 1962 when Warrant Officer Frans Loots was sent to Holland to learn how to train and handle Police patrol dogs. Tracker dogs had been in use for some time in rural areas prior to the police realising that patrol dogs could assist in catching fleeing fugitive along with tracking and finding items of evidence. Patrol dogs were then trained and deployed to major cities.

As a white boy in my last year at school, I received my national service call up papers assigning me to an army unit in Bloemfontein for basic training of nine months. My liberal parents did not like the idea of their eldest son having to do National Service in the Army. The options were to delay the service by further study, to risk prosecution by not reporting or to move to another country; none of which appealed to me or the family.

Whilst considering my National Service options one night after
10pm I heard breaking glass, so went to my bedroom window and
looked out towards the corner store. An alarm went off and I saw
two figures run down the road from the direction of the store. A
few minutes later a large Ford Galaxy police squad car with a dog
in the back arrived at speed, mounting the large grass covered
centre island. The policeman's dog quickly picked up scent near
the broken window and followed spoor down the road in the
direction that the men had run.

This incident planted a seed in my mind.

The two Durban daily newspapers reported frequently on arrests
by the Police Flying Squad and Dog Unit for a range of offences
extending from robberies and housebreakings to stolen car chases.
The Dog Unit were the glamour boys and were well regarded by
the public at large.

My father made some enquiries and the option of doing my
National Service in the Police seemed like the best way forward.

In pre television South Africa most families listened to Springbok
Radio as their source of evening entertainment. Probably one of
the most popular radio programmes ever broadcast was Squad
Cars; a dramatized story of the South African Police at work. The
series started in June 1968 on Friday nights in the 7.30pm slot and
it came to an end in June 1985 as the attraction of TV drew
listeners away. South Africans will remember the opening intro-
duction before each episode;

"The story you are about to hear is true. Details are supplied from
official case files from the South African Police; only names and places
have been changed to protect innocent people involved.

General Motors brings you the drama, the danger, the facts, as the
long arm of the law travel in squad cars.

They prowl the empty streets at night, waiting, in fast cars, on foot,
living with crime and violence, these men are on duty 24 hours out of
every 24, they face danger at every turn, expecting nothing less, they
protect the people of South Africa, these are the men of Squad Cars".

Policing in the 1970s never had the technology and forensic tools available today, other than fingerprints. There was no DNA or the ability to track people through mobile phones or to examine computers to recover key items of evidence. There were no sophisticated police data bases or programmes to rapidly access information to help the policeman at the scene of a crime. Police cars were not fitted with sirens, flashing blue lights or even hazard lights, and the police radio was fixed in the car or van. Once you walked into a complaint you were on your own with no access to information or the ability to call for assistance. A list of stolen cars was maintained manually and kept on a Card Index at Police Radio Station, so instinct, gut feel, experience, and being fully alert were vital to compensate for the lack of technology.

Detectives had heavy caseloads so without fingerprints or information about suspects, cases were closed as undetected. The Dog Unit realised that we had the best chance of catching criminals during or shortly after the commission of a crime when evidence or stolen property was available.

Cases are drawn from old press clippings and experiences of determinedly racing to crimes in progress, highlighting the dangers faced daily to catch the crooks and protect the public.

The book is contextualised in terms of South African society and politics at the time and emphasises the cohesiveness of the Dog Unit and the relationship, loyalty and commitment between dog and Handler.

A special thank you to former Dog Unit colleagues Vince Zimmerman, Doug Linden and Mervin Van Rensburg for sharing their cases with me as well as photographs and press clippings. Thanks to my wife, Debbie, for help in reviewing many of the cases and countless drafts.

I dedicate this book not only to the Durban Dog Handlers of the 1970's but all those who served from the beginning in 1962 to the present day, especially in memory of those who lost their lives or were injured in the line of duty. Thanks to all those comrades whose support and steadfast courage in the face of danger made Durban a safer place.
We were always there to back up one another.

Map of Durban and Surrounding Suburbs

1

LIFE AS A STUDENT CONSTABLE

My father made enquiries with the Police Recruitment office and established that I could do my National Service in the Police albeit with a longer period of service to fulfil my commitment. There were several positives with this option. Basic training would be 6 months in Pretoria with a greater academic focus on law and police procedures, a posting back to Durban to serve a further 3 years, and a reasonable salary compared to the basic pay for Military National Service. Dad thought that this also could lead to a legal career on leaving if I felt that way inclined.

I attended an interview with the Police Recruitment Officer, submitted fingerprints, underwent some psychometric tests and a medical examination after meeting the height and chest measurement requirement. I produced a favourable school reference and one from my Scout Master and was later informed that I would be accepted. I wrote my school Matric exams and presented myself just a few days later at the Recruitment Office to start as a Student Constable on 17 December 1968.

When I arrived in the Police Recruitment offices, I met Doug Linden who I recognised from school. Sergeant Delaney gave us some papers and told us to go to the old Durban Central Police station in Smith Street to see Captain O'Connell who would attest us and then send us both off to the Umbilo Police Station as we lived in the area. We would be Student Constables in plain clothes at Umbilo until July 1969 when we would go to Police College in Pretoria for the six month course. After the brief attestation process, we were told to report to the Station Commander, Warrant Officer Johnny Small at Umbilo Police Station in Deodar Avenue.

Johnny Small was in his fifties and had a row of Second World War medal ribbons on his tunic. He was an Afrikaans speaker, but his English was good albeit with a strong accent as was the case with most Afrikaners who had lived in Durban for some time. Doug, who had already turned 18, would be attached to a shift in the Charge Office. As I was only 17 years old, I could not work shifts, so he called Sergeant Albert Van Reenen into his office. Albert was already retired and was working as a Temporary Sergeant in charge of the Uniform Accident and Enquiry Section and had an even more impressive row of World War II medal ribbons.

There were already 3 other Student Constables at the station and there was now a student on each of the 4 shifts with me the baby, on a day job.

I was taken into the Accident and Enquiry office which housed 4 or 5 desks. I was allocated a desk and shown the form SAP 352 which was used to report motor vehicle accidents. The method of completing the form was shown to me and I watched as Constable Dave Roux filled the first few reports from members of the public. The form was large and had to be filled in quadruplicate which meant having to use 3 sheets of carbon paper. This was to be my job for the next six and a half months. On rainy days I could complete 8 to 10 reports and have people lined up waiting.

The Police environment was a real education. The other members of the unit would execute warrants and summonses as well as trace witnesses and take statements. I helped in all these areas and did everything short of leaving the office due to my age restriction. The overall staff compliment of the station was really very small considering the size of the area and levels of crime. Each of the 4 Charge Office shifts comprised a Charge Office Sergeant with 1 or 2 African Constables, or as they were called at the time, Bantu Constable Charge Office Reserves, and a White Constable van driver with a Bantu Constable van crew. The van would attend to complaints and reports received in the area and would cover other areas as the vans were equipped with radios and received their complaints from Police Radio Control.

The Detective Unit comprised the Branch Commander, Detective Sergeant MW Pretorius who was in his early 40's, plus 2 or 3 white detectives and 3 non-white detectives. Detective Sergeant Sam Naidoo was a very experienced and competent detective who could handle any sort of investigation ranging from murder to fraud. A lot of his work originated from the King Edward Hospital.

When there was nothing going on in the Accident and Enquiry Office, I would visit the detectives. I would watch them interviewing complainants, witnesses and suspects, and observed how they changed their questioning techniques and approach depending on the matter in hand or the persons they were interviewing. They looked for facts, proofs and evidence to substantiate allegations.

I realised that I needed to be confident and assertive when situations required. Just the fact that you are a policeman gives one an air of authority and most people will comply with what you tell them if you have a confident bearing and attitude. I was quick to watch and learn techniques of handling various situations, but I had to learn how to adopt the air of confidence which was a challenge when only a few months earlier I sat in a classroom being compliant and polite.

The detectives would investigate cases where suspects had been arrested by members of the Dog Unit, either by patrolling crime affected areas or by responding to reports of crime in progress. Cases included housebreaking of residential, commercial and industrial premises, robberies and stolen cars, often after high speed chases. When a dog car stopped at the Station, I would ask who the Dog Handlers were. I was told stories of serious case arrests by Sergeant Fred Pautz and his dog Caro, Constable Manie Odendaal and Prins, and Constable Phillip Sonnekus and Rex. All three dogs were household names that had received the Police Medal of Honour for courage and faithfulness. This was what I wanted to do but I had some growing up and learning to do.

———

In early July 1969, around 30 Student Constables from Durban and I took the train to Pretoria. We were met by a Drill Sergeant who shouted at everybody until we got into large trucks and were taken to the Police Training College. We stood on the parade ground until our names were called out and we were marched off with our bags to a barrack room. We were designated Troop 30 which was an English-speaking group so our training and lectures would be in English. With around 1000 students under training, we were the only English troop in the new intake.

Our training included an emphasis on law, police procedures and investigation of crime techniques and processes with regular written tests. There was also firearm training with a .38 revolver, shotgun and the FN self-loading rifle (SLR). Parade ground drill and gym work with an emphasis on self-defence and boxing was helpful in developing self-confidence and being able to handle ourselves if a criminal resisted arrest. Five and a half months later we wrote exams to obtain a National Senior Certificate in law subjects and attended a passing out parade at the Pretoria rugby stadium. The training was concentrated and very relevant to what waited for us as fully-fledged policemen. I had grown up during my time away from home and had made the transition from a boy to a young man having lost 15 pounds in weight whilst growing a further 2 inches.

Most of the Durban contingent was posted back to Durban and we were met by senior officers who assigned us to various stations. Doug Linden and I were posted back to Umbilo. Before we were sent off back to our stations, we were briefed on the work of his unit by Captain Dan Van Wyk who was the Commander of the Murder and Robbery Squad. He asked who had seen a dead body and explained that the first exposure to a serious incident involving a body might be difficult, and the shock could result in failing to secure the crime scene and take charge of evidence. We were then taken to the Police Mortuary and given a tour of the fridges with briefings about circumstances relating to the deaths of some of the bodies. It was in effect, a forensic briefing.

What really struck me was the smell of disinfectant and cold air that hit me when the fridge door was opened. It was gruesome yet informative and effective. I nervously looked at the bodies, some of which were badly mutilated. I had mixed feelings of fear and curiosity that I was trying to manage in a professional way. I remembered my dad had always said that we have nothing to fear from dead people and I suppose that was when I lost what was left of my boyhood.

Van Wyk pointed out that it would be embarrassing if one of us were despatched to a fatal accident and the public had to phone and ask for another policeman to attend because the man on the scene was getting sick, or crying and unable to manage to the scene.

2

LEARNING THE ROPES

I was assigned to the Charge Office where duties included dealing with the public who came in to report crimes or ask for advice, report accidents or other general enquiries. The station had 3 temporary holding cells for persons who had been arrested and would be held until the next court date. On occasion, some charged persons would be remanded back to the cells for ongoing investigations which could include the recovery of stolen property, visits to the crime scene, or assisting in finding other suspects still at large.

Constable Andries Van Der Walt was the senior member of the shift who drove the police van accompanied by another Constable as crew, to attend complaints reported by the public. Most complaints were made to the Police Radio Control who directed the station vans to various places usually with details of the nature of the complaint, the address and a name of the complainant. Radio Control would then assign the complaint to the closest available vehicle. For minor complaints it was usually the station van that was dispatched, whilst for serious cases the Dog Handlers were first responders. At shift change, the Van Driver who was going off duty would fill up with petrol and sign the vehicle back into a vehicle register. The Van Driver of the oncoming shift would inspect the vehicle for damage and check the oil, water and tyre pressure. The senior member would inspect all members of the shift to ensure that uniform and equipment was in order.

When I returned to Umbilo after College our standard firearm was the .38 Smith and Wesson revolver which took 6 rounds. The firearm was in a holster as part of a Sam Brown belt and cross strap over the shoulder with a lanyard under the shoulder epaulette attached to the revolver, so it was connected to the policeman and did not fall out when running, and would not be easily removed in a scuffle. We also had a handcuff pouch and a baton that fitted into a deep left side trouser pocket. The van driver wrote up his pocketbook with details of complaints or incidents which usually was attached to a clipboard with blank case dockets and foolscap paper for taking statements. A good four battery torch was essential equipment for the van driver especially on a night shift, or in the late afternoon.

———

One afternoon around sunset, Van Der Walt took a phone call from a house about 100 metres away from the Police Station reporting that a vacant house across the road had been vandalised. As he was about to attend another complaint, he suggested that I should walk around the corner to Frere Road to chat with the complainant. On my arrival at the address, the complainant reported that an elderly neighbour had passed away some months earlier and that her furniture and other goods had been moved out by the family, but the house had been vacant for some time. Torch or candle lights were seen in the house from time to time. The complainant clearly wanted me to go over and brief him on what I found. I realised immediately that I did not have a torch with me and whilst it was still dusk, the light was fading fast. I decided against going back to the station to get a torch and went through the unlocked front door of the vacant house.

It was lot darker inside the house than I expected, and I

paused to let my eyes get accustomed to the gloom. I was hoping that the streetlights would give me some visibility so I could see what level of vandalism, if any had taken place. The lounge and dining room had some newspaper on the floor which led me to believe that someone may be sleeping there from time to time. I went into the kitchen which seemed OK and then into a passage leading to the bedrooms and bathroom. This area was quite a lot darker than the lounge area, so I stopped and listened for any sound of any other persons in the house. As I was only out of College a few weeks at the time, I was not as experienced or confident as I would become later. I felt tension rising and I considered going back to the complainant and telling him that all was in order and to contact the family of the owner the next day to arrange to secure the house. That would have been a "cop out" and I was determined to go through with this despite a sense of unease.

I came to a partially open bedroom door and peered into a pitch-black room. I stopped and listened and then stepped into the room and at that moment I felt someone grab hold of my lanyard and jerk me backwards. I shat myself! I pulled away, shouted out and kicked in the direction of where I expected my attacker to be. I kicked into fresh air, then realised that I had caught my lanyard on the door handle. There was no one in the house. I composed myself and went back to the complainant and reported all was clear.

I learnt two important lessons; to take a torch even if you go into poorly lit areas by day and to ensure that, wherever possible, for two policemen to attend even the most routine complaint as things can escalate. It would also be difficult to refute any allegations if unaccompanied. We were expected to work in pairs, but circumstances would arise when we would find ourselves alone and we had to be alert knowing that we could be at risk.

During my first year at Umbilo, I was exposed to a lot of relatively petty crime, domestic disputes, as well as some serious crime. Many of the issues were dealt with very mechanically, showing a degree of empathy when necessary, but never taking too deep a personal interest in a problem. I believed that if I took to heart every complaint I attended, I would probably have become an emotional wreck within a week. Despite this defence mechanism, there were situations which touched us and left some form of emotional fingerprint. One such case that made an impact was one of a runaway schoolgirl.

A family living in a good area near Nicholson Road had adopted a baby girl and brought her up as their own child. When she was about 15 or 16 years of age, she found out that she was adopted, and became unstable and difficult at home and at school. After some weeks of this behaviour she ran away from home. Her parents came to the station and reported her missing. We had her photo in the Information book but nothing much else to follow. We shift workers would be on the lookout for her whilst we continued to attend complaints and deal with other regular police duties.

This sort of case would usually be investigated by the Uniform Investigation Unit, but as that only consisted of Sergeant Albert Van Reenen and 2 other Constables who would be dealing with issuing summons, warrants of arrest and accident investigations, the chance of this missing person getting much time without specific clues was decidedly low. The parents were tireless in their own efforts, putting notices up in shopping centres and phoned us regularly. This was a time before we had properly established processes and techniques for recording and investigating missing persons and the success or otherwise came down to the ability of the parents to appeal to individual policemen and the time we had between complaints.

One evening about a week after the girl went missing, just as I was about to go off duty, a woman phoned the station and said that she had some information. Constable Schoeman, who was coming on duty and I went to Flamingo Court to meet with our informant. Flamingo Court was a very large block of Council flats about 12 stories tall and consisted of over 200 individual flats. At that time the residents were all Whites from the lower socio-economic group. Many of the households comprised single parent households with lots of kids and some older families that had fallen on hard times through illness or unemployment. The informant was a young married woman who was probably about 20 years old with 2 young children. Her husband was an artisan and he worked irregular hours. She told us that she had met the girl and had brought her into her top floor flat. The girl was not there at the time of our visit. She had realised that the girl was missing as she had poured her heart out to her. She had convinced the girl that she would need to contact her parents. The girl was reluctant to do this, so the woman had contacted the police.

She asked us to leave the matter until the following day, by which time she would arrange for the girl to contact her parents. We had to decide whether to leave the matter as suggested or to try to find the girl and take her to her parents. We decided to go with the woman's suggestion. We then chatted generally, and it appeared to me that she was taken with Schoeman and seemed to be up for a brief encounter. We left the flat and contacted the parents and gave them feedback about our visit. The runaway contacted her parents the next day; they met and arranged for professional counselling. That seemed to be the end of another routine police matter, but it had a climax about 2 or 3 months later.

Early one evening I was called to attend to a report that a woman had fallen to her death down the stairwell at Flamingo Court. On my arrival, I went to the ground floor stairwell area and saw the body of a woman in a pool of blood. Her body was lying in a contorted manner and it was obvious that she had broken just about every bone in her body. She had fallen from the top floor and had hit and bounced off ledges on the way down. The ambulance staff and flat supervisor were standing by, so I spoke to some of the residents who related that she had an argument with her husband and had run out the flat and down the passage towards the stairs. She had either fallen or jumped down the stairwell to her death. I was satisfied by various reports that she had not been pushed by anyone. I then asked to be taken to her flat. It was only when I walked into the flat that I realised the dead woman was our informant in the case of the runaway schoolgirl. It came as a bit of a shock to me. I had seen dead bodies before but there had never been any personal knowledge of the victim. The dead woman was so badly damaged that I had not recognised her. That possible suicide or accident introduced me to a new dimension of knowing the victim, and this took a little mental readjustment to keep it just another routine police incident.

———

The night shift came on duty at 9pm so when I finished an after-noon shift, I would occasionally stay on duty for 2 or 3 hours and join the night shift van driver to get more experience in attending complaints and crime scenes. When Dog Handlers from the Flying Squad stopped off at Umbilo, I was quick to offer a cup of tea or coffee and chat about how they worked with their dog, and relationships developed. I would arrange to crew on a dog car with Constable Flip Sonnekus on a night shift from time to time and learnt a lot about police processes and personal styles in dealing with the public.

Sonnekus and Rex had been partners since 1965 when they completed their training at the Police Dog School in Pretoria. Flip lived in an old style flat in Fenniscowles Road, Umbilo, and Rex lived there with the family, on a large balcony. Dog and handler were well known not just in Police circles but to the general public as well. The two Durban daily newspapers followed the exploits and cases of the Dog Unit and that, together with the Squad Cars programme on Springbok radio on Friday nights, made some of the unit minor celebrities. The relationship between the police and public was very positive. We were in the public eye and did not wish to disappoint.

Rex had been awarded the South African Police Medal of Honour for Courage and Faithfulness in 1967. The Medal was insti-tuted in 1963, and by 2001 when it was discontinued there had been 33 awards with 12 of them awarded to members of the Durban Dog Unit.

· · ·

Detectives would often ask for members of the Dog Unit to accompany them when seeking to arrest criminals for serious cases to give them an extra capability, especially if the suspect fled the scene. In February 1967, Detectives from the Murder and Robbery Squad received information that a suspect wanted for murder and armed robbery was at a house north of the city in the Kwa Mashu Township. The suspect was believed to be armed with a firearm, so the Detectives requested that Sonnekus and Rex accompany them. They arrived at the address around 3am and tried to gain entry however this alerted the suspect who threatened to shoot anyone who tried to enter. The Detectives forced windows at various points of the house and whilst they called out to the man to distract him, Rex was lifted through a window to attack the suspect. Shortly afterwards shouts were heard, and the police stormed into the house and saw Rex and the suspect engaged in an almighty fight. Sonnekus overpowered the man and found a loaded .25 pistol in his pocket.

When Rex grabbed onto the man, he tried to beat the dog off with a spade, but Rex continued his attack and the man was too busy fighting off the dog and was unable to draw his weapon before he was tackled by Sonnekus. The dogs' courage and continued determination in not flinching or giving way meant the arrest was carried out without loss of life or serious injury.

———

Night shift in the charge office never followed a pattern as it could be very busy or really uneventful. I always took a book to read on night shifts if things were quiet and spoke with Constable Simon Mbali who had 14 years' service and was a source of much wisdom. I asked him about African customs and life in the cities and in the traditional tribal areas and he gave me a better understanding of Black aspirations and hardships.

I learned the routine of dealing with a range of telephonic

complaints or enquiries, and how to process suspects and visit the cells every hour. Two Policemen would visit the cells every hour and enquire if everything was in order. I also learnt to watch the body language to see if any prisoner was molesting any of the others and to check if there were any attempts at escape or self-harm. I realised early on that whilst one may have a prisoner in the cell for a relatively minor charge, one could not expect them all to be docile. Some prisoners may have committed other more serious crimes than that for which they had been detained. A fingerprint record check may reveal other outstanding crimes, so a person arrested for a petty crime could not be taken too lightly. I had heard stories of policemen who had been attacked and injured or killed by apparently petty criminals.

One evening at about midnight, the van driver of the neighbouring police station at Mayville, brought an African man into the Charge Office and asked me to hold him there until 4am. It was an offence against a Provincial Proclamation for Africans to walk about in a "White Area" between 11pm and 4am. The man had lost control of his car and driven into the hedge of the Durban Girls High School. He had been drinking but the policeman decided that as the hedge was not severely damaged and the car only had a damaged tyre rim with scratches on the body work, that he would not arrest him or charge him. The man sat in a holding area and was agitated. He asked Mbali if he could go. Mbali said that he had to stay there until 4am to avoid being arrested for curfew. He kept up his badgering and after about an hour, Mbali told me that the man was being a nuisance and maybe we should let him go and take his chances. We had no right to hold him as no charge had been laid, so we told him to leave if he wished.

About an hour later, the Mayville policeman came rushing into the Charge Office looking for the driver. He had discovered that the car had been stolen as the owner had reported it missing and he was now looking for the thief. He felt very sheepish as he should have checked the registration details of the vehicle and paid attention to the ignition or key used to start the car. A check for documents in the cubby hole or in the car may also have given some information about the owner. That may not have been as stupid in those days as it may seem today. Vehicle registration details were not readily available. Durban registration details after office hours could only be obtained by going to the City Police offices to get a key for the Licensing Offices to then look up the card index for the name and address of owners which would then require someone to go to the address and make enquiries.

By mid-1970 I was assigned as van driver to attend complaints and general duties. Weekdays during office hours had a number of station admin duties but the weekends and night shifts focussed on complaints and crime and that was what interested me. I had only been driving the van for a few weeks when late one Sunday afternoon I finished dealing with a minor complaint and as it was shift hand over time, I dropped my crew at the bus rank to get home. I then headed back to the station when I received a call from Radio Control. I was asked to attend an accident in Essenwood Road in the Berea police area. It appeared that I was the only one available as the Berea van was at the station with the handover. I reluctantly agreed to go without my crew but as I expected that it was a minor accident I hoped I could get the drivers to exchange personal details and go the Berea Station and make a report.

As I approached the area, I saw 2 vehicles blocking the road and a crowd on the pavement. Some people were holding a man and as I got out of the van a woman handed me a Webley .38 revolver and indicated that the man who was being restrained had been in possession of the weapon. I took the revolver, searched the man and placed him in the back of the van. The crowd then drifted off and I was left with a suspect, a firearm that was probably illegal or stolen and no chain of evidence from witnesses. Things had happened too fast to get that detail. I took the suspect off to the Berea Charge Office and made a statement to open a case for possession of an unlicensed firearm. I hoped and expected that the Detectives from Berea would follow the case up and get more detailed evidence. The Detectives had 48 hours to either charge or release the suspect.

A couple of months later I received a subpoena to attend the Regional Court rather than a Magistrate's Court which meant that the accused probably had previous convictions or the Detectives had linked the man or firearm to outstanding cases. I had received no further feedback from the Detectives about the progress of the investigation since the date of the incident. I got to court early and looked through the police docket and saw that the accused had several earlier convictions including the previous possession of an unlicensed firearm. The Berea Detectives had made no effort to trace any other witnesses. I gave my evidence and the accused, who conducted his own defence, began to cross examine me. His questions to me were good, as one would expect from an old jail-bird. He asked me if I saw him in possession of the firearm. I said I did not as the weapon was given to me by a woman bystander. He then asked if the woman was present in court to give evidence and I admitted that she was not. He then told the Magistrate that he was innocent, and that he was being framed with no evidence to link him with the firearm.

The Magistrate summed up the evidence before making his finding. He correctly pointed out that the evidence was incomplete, and that the investigation was poor. He found the man not guilty and the accused walked out of court with a sneer in my direction. This was my first real arrest and the man was found not guilty because of poor police work. If I had a crew with me things may have been different. I was really annoyed because I expected more help from the Detectives. I had learnt another valuable lesson. Evidence not obtained at the scene of the crime is often irreplaceable. If I got to a crime scene first, then I would be in charge and it was up to me to ask for backup if required. The Detectives' failure should have been a disciplinary matter as there appeared to be no follow up on the original or legal owner or whether the weapon had been linked to other criminal cases through ballistic tests. I determined that in future I would follow those things up before it was set down for court because I would be the idiot in the witness box. I promised myself that I would not let that happen to me again, and it very rarely ever did for the rest of my police career.

Looking back, what was expected at that time of a uniform policeman at a scene of a crime was rather onerous. In most countries, a uniform policeman would only be expected to secure a serious crime scene until detectives or other specialists arrived. In those days a detective from the station would be on standby for a call out after hours but rarely came out unless it a very serious matter such as a robbery with a shooting involved, or a murder was reported. It was up to the uniformed policemen to deal with the matter and the Radio Control Duty Officer who also worked shifts could be called in for guidance after normal office hours.

My first year after Police College was an interesting and testing time, not just for what I learned through successful cases, but also through what I got wrong as an individual or through colleagues' experiences.

One Saturday afternoon as I was about to go off duty from my morning shift, the van driver of the oncoming shift took a phone call from one of the Detectives who asked him to arrest a suspect in a fraud case. The detectives had investigated a case where a Director of a transport and shipping company down on the Maydon Wharf had defrauded the company of a large sum of money. The case had been in court and the Director had been found guilty. He was to remain on bail on remand for a few weeks before the Magistrate passed sentence. A prison sentence was the likely outcome; however, he jumped bail and did not appear in court. The detectives had been to his house to arrest him several times, but his wife said that he had left, and she did not know where he was. The Investigating Officer told my colleague that he had received information that the fugitive was at home and he asked us to arrest him. He also cautioned that the man was very deceitful and that his family would do anything to assist him. As we jumped into the van, I asked my colleague who took the call for more details and a description of the man. He said he was described as being in his late forties, of average height and build with brownish coloured hair. Not entirely helpful.

We parked the van a distance away from the house and approached on foot. As we walked up the path to the front door, I decided to go around the back and stood on a bank in the back garden with a view of the back door and the windows on both sides of the house in case he made a run for it. After a minute the back door opened. A man took a few steps into the yard and then looked up at me. He seemed quite calm and indicated for me to come down. I followed him into the house. My colleague who was taking the lead on this matter was speaking in Afrikaans to two women and the man who fitted the general description. I understood the conversation, but my Afrikaans was still to develop considerably over the years to fluency in speaking, reading and writing. The occupants of the house denied that the man was our suspect, and he claimed to be the brother in law of the wife and husband of the second woman. My colleague was undecided about what we should do. We asked for identity documents, but the man said that he was visiting and did not have any with him. We asked him to accompany us to the police station to verify his identity, but he asked if he was being arrested and he wanted his lawyer present. My colleague was not prepared to take the risk of having allegations of unlawful arrest made against him and he had no means of contacting the detective, so he decided to leave the house. When we got back to the station, he phoned the detective and related the events at the house. It became clear that the man was our suspect, so we went back to the house to find that he had disappeared.

I felt really stupid about the whole thing. The detective should have come out with us as he could identify the man, and my colleague should have got a better description of our man. If we went to the house without the detective, my colleague should have taken a phone number to contact the detective for guidance on how to proceed. The whole episode was unprofessional and incompetent and the only saving grace was that the case was not a serious "life and death" case.

Some 6 months later one of my uniform colleagues, Kevin Moran, went to a flat where the wife was living at around 4am and found a man with the wife. Both denied that he was our accused and were quite convincing. Kevin knew about our failed episode, so he took the man to the station and called the detectives out to confirm his identity. He was the man. He had been on the run for several months, had travelled to family in Johannesburg and had also slept rough in Durban parks. It may have been better for him to have gone to jail rather than put himself through such hardship and heavy spending to keep on the run.

The Police had a system of using Reservists who were civilian volunteers trained on the job, issued with uniforms, and awarded rank on ability and service. Umbilo had an active group of about 9 or 10 Reservists who would take over the Police Station and Van Driver duties on one weekend a month. They would usually cover 3 shifts from Saturday afternoon, the night shift and the Sunday morning. Some would come into the station on a mid-week evening and chat or crew on the van for a few hours attending various complaints. I enjoyed working with the Reservists as I found their diverse backgrounds interesting. Many longer serving policemen did not like Reservists at all. They argued that as long as Reservists were prepared to work for nothing and supplement the manpower requirement, we would never get a decent pay increase.

On one Reservist takeover, the van with a driver and 2 crew members were called to a housebreaking in Carrington Heights shortly before midnight. The family had gone out to a movie and on their return found that the house had been broken into and items had been packed ready for removal. They had obviously disturbed the suspects and the Reservists were at the house within minutes of the call. They parked the van in the front driveway and went into the house to look around and to take a statement. One of the Reservists remained in the van to listen to the radio which was fixed in the vehicle. That was standard practice as members outside the vehicle had no communication on their person to remain in touch with the Radio Control to receive complaints or to call for aid. Removable or portable radios that could be used on a charger in the vehicle and then taken out to the scene of the crime only became available a few years later.

The Reservist in the van became bored with sitting in the van so he got out and walked towards a bush to relieve himself. He was in full stream when suddenly a man who had been hiding in the bush jumped out and ran off making good his escape. The suspect had initially not been able to get away unseen because when the family returned home, the husband went into the house to phone the police when they discovered the front door open and the rest of the family waited in the front garden. The Reservists were mostly middle aged civic minded men who lacked the fitness and probably the resolve to run after a suspect, overpower him and arrest him.

The story was often told and retold at the station with the eventual version alleging that the suspect was prepared to endure being peed on but when the reservist began to break wind, he thought that the policeman was going to crap on him, so he then took off down the road.

————

In late 1970, the Station Commander called me in and told me that he had been instructed by District Headquarters to second a Constable to Radio Control for about a month because they were understaffed. I was assigned to a shift which comprised a Warrant Officer or a Senior Sergeant as the Indoor Supervisor, about 4 or 5 Constables, and 1 or 2 female Clerical Assistants. It was our job to receive calls direct from the public on the police emergency number as well as to take complaints from about 20 Police Stations in the Durban area to pass on to their vans by radio. Each shift had a Duty Officer, usually a Lieutenant who was responsible for the Radio Control indoor staff. The Duty Officer provided oversight of the Dog Unit cars, the station Charge Office staff, and van drivers after normal office hours. He would be informed of any serious cases and decide if higher authority needed to be informed, plus deal with press enquiries, and any complaints against the police.

I found the work interesting. My time as a van driver had made me a good interrogator of complainants so I would get all the pertinent information from the caller that a policeman would need when he arrived at a complaint or the scene of the crime. This was particularly important as new recruits from other parts of the country were often posted to Radio Control, their English was poor, and they often spelt the names of streets incorrectly which wasted time whilst clarity of the actual address was having to be confirmed. The civilian clerical assistants were generally fairly good after they had been at the job for some time. If a complaint was not accurately passed on to a patrol car or van or with very sketchy or inaccurate information, it could have serious consequences for policemen despatched to the scene.

An example of passing on complaints without obtaining sufficient information almost had fatal consequences for a Dog Unit Constable. A man had been convicted of a series of robberies and had been sentenced to a long term of imprisonment. He was arrested in the first instance because his wife had co-operated with the Detectives. He was placed on a train in Durban with a prison guard to be transported to the Pretoria Central Prison. During the train journey, he overpowered the guard taking his revolver and making good his escape when the train stopped at a station. He returned to his wife's home in Florida Road as he had a score to settle with her. The wife was able to alert a neighbour that her husband had arrived, and Radio Control was contacted. The person who received the call did not know what to make of the call. Complaints were usually prefixed with a code number such as code 4 for a robbery, code 8 for disturbance, and so on. This call had aspects of escaped prisoner, possession of a firearm, hostage taking and such like. So after some pondering, the complaint was passed on to the Despatcher as a disturbance complaint between a husband and wife.

The policeman drove straight up to the address in his police car and parked in full view of the house. He got out, opened the front gate and was walking up the path when the front door opened with the escapee pointing a revolver and firing at him. The policeman instinctively drew his revolver as he moved to cover and returned fire. The door slammed shut and the policeman ran to the car to call for back up. Several Police vehicles arrived within minutes and they carefully approached the house from all sides. The escapers' wife opened the front door and told the Police that her husband had been wounded and had run into the bathroom. The policemen went to the bathroom and listened carefully at the door. They called out to the escapee, but he did not reply. They heard a grunting noise and forced the door open. The escapee had been shot in the throat and was badly injured. An ambulance was called but the escapee was declared dead on arrival at hospital.

3

PROMOTION TO SERGEANT

In early 1971 a Police circular was distributed outlining the curriculum for that year's promotion exam to Sergeant. The key aspect for me was that the age restriction of 21 was rescinded and replaced with 2 years' service and successfully passing the exams. The curriculum included 8 subjects but as I had already passed my Law Matric in Police College which covered much of the syllabus, I would only be required to write 2 papers on Police Administration and Standing Orders, and a paper on Investigation of Crime. I submitted my application to write the exams and requested 2 weeks leave to cram the syllabus. When a colleague heard that I was going to write my exams, he suggested that I should rather not write the exam. He had written exams in previous years but was unsuccessful on each occasion. He suggested that I should rather be a clever Constable than a stupid Sergeant. I responded by saying that I intended to be a clever Sergeant. I wrote my exams and passed and was advised that my promotion was to be effective from 1 July 1971. I was still about 4 months away from my 20th birthday. I was issued with my stripes and my proud mother sewed them on to my uniforms.

The Police had a system where promotion meant transfer. It

was a very good system that posted a newly promoted policeman to a new Station or role, so they left their friends and colleagues and started fresh without any of the old friendships or familiarities. I was informed that I would be posted to Stamford Hill Station effective 1 January 1972. Stamford Hill was about 5 or 6 kilometres away and had a similar profile to Umbilo of White residential areas with affluent households closer to the ridge moving to middle class and working class the closer one got to Umgeni Road. Umgeni Road was a main arterial route for traffic from the North of Durban towards the centre of town and had a large number of commercial and industrial properties. The area around Umgeni Road had a number of big and small Indian businesses, and was a busy and mostly prosperous area.

As it happened, I still had a couple of months to work at Umbilo until the transfer took place. The change of status from a young Constable to Sergeant was met with mixed reactions. The Station Commander was genuinely sorry to see me go, especially as he knew the poor reputation of the Sergeant who was to be posted to replace me. Most of my colleagues were pleased for me whilst others were indifferent or a little put out.

I continued to work at Umbilo until the end of the year as the shift van driver and occasionally worked in the Charge Office. A Student Constable, Charles Van Der Merwe, was assigned to my shift. He had left school about 3 years earlier and had already completed his National Service in the Army. His sister was going out with a policeman, so he decided to join the Police as it seemed a good career choice to him. One Sunday afternoon when I had been wearing my stripes for less than a week, I was on the van and had Charles with me as crew. Students were not expected to be exposed to situations that may have an element of risk, but Charles was mature and physically strong, and Sunday shifts were usually quiet. We got a call around 5pm to go to a block of flats just off Point Road to attend to a disturbance complaint. We were advised that the son of the complainant had been drinking and tried to commit suicide by jumping out the window of the sixth floor flat.

Promoted to Sergeant 1971

On our arrival, other residents of the flats alerted by the noise directed us to the roof where the young man had run, pursued by his parents and neighbours. We took the lift to the top floor and ran up the last flight of stairs to the roof. We were unprepared for the sight that awaited us. The would-be suicide victim was in his early 20's and was dressed only in a pair of jeans. He was a bear of a man who had tried to jump through the flat's lounge window without opening it and had several large cuts on his head and chest area. It was like a horror movie. It looked as though a bucket of blood had been poured over him. He had tried to jump off the roof and was being constrained by his family and several others. I went straight to him and took his arm. He stopped struggling and started to cry which made me feel more comfortable that he was not going to pursue his intention of jumping off the roof.

I told Charles to run to the van and radio for an ambulance. I spoke to the man in a caring but authoritative manner saying that we were going to get him to hospital and then discuss his problems. The family and neighbours went down the stairs ahead of me as I started to guide him towards the stairs and asked if I could do anything else for him. He suddenly erupted and said that he wanted to die and that I was going with him. He rushed me to the edge of the building about 10 levels above ground and tried to throw us both off. I swung myself around to get behind him and to loosen his grip, at the same time lowering my centre of gravity. I tipped him over me in a judo throw and jumped on top of him twisting his arm behind his back. He was still struggling desperately and trying to drag himself towards the edge a few feet away. He cried out, "I want to die!", and I cried out silently to myself that I wanted to live whilst I increased the pressure on his arm. Neighbours alerted by the shouts came back onto the roof and grabbed hold of him as he began to sob and relax. Charles returned and we got him down and into the back of the van with handcuffs securely fitted.

I drove the 2 blocks to the large Addington Hospital casualty reception area. I was sweating profusely from the exertion and shock and was covered in his blood. When we got into the hospital, the staff wanted to treat me first as they thought that I was badly injured. The intern doctor on duty in casualty was my former classmate and Dux of the school, Lawrence Usher. He and the nurses cleaned me up and stitched the injured man, then arranged for a psychiatrist to examine him and liaise with his family.

My uniform was covered in blood and I had to go home to change. I walked into the house and quickly reassured my parents that I had not been hurt even though I looked a fright with blood all over me and my uniform. I had a lucky escape because my reflexes were good, but I realised I had probably relaxed too soon when the situation was not yet totally under control. The man was very strong, but I had found reserves of strength, and good wrestling and judo techniques to save myself from a potentially fatal situation. That lesson and many others like that would develop my ability to read a situation and keep control.

———

I arrived at Stamford Hill in early January 1972 and was briefed by the Station Commander, Captain Nel. I was to be one of four Shift Leaders and Charge Office Sergeants. Gert Van Den Berg was one of the shift Sergeants whom I had spoken to on the phone when I was based at Umbilo. He had started his career at Umbilo and his mother still lived in the area. Gert was to become a lifelong friend and had been in the police for around 10 years. I also met Constable Piet Van Der Merwe who was about to move from the uniform branch to the CID. Both Piet and Gert had a history that was linked to a significant dog and handler arrest.

In early September 1965 Piet Van Der Merwe was patrolling in a van in the Warwick Avenue area with a colleague in the early hours of the morning. The area was home to the bus ranks that came in from the African townships of Kwa Mashu in the North and Umlazi in the South as well as the Indian Market, and Fish Market area. This area started to come alive around 5am and it was usual to look out for criminals who had been involved in house-breakings and robberies overnight who would look to catch a bus back to their homes with their stolen goods. The Berea Road railway station was also located in the general area.

Piet and his colleague spotted two men who were carrying heavy boxes and suitcases. They stopped the van near them with the intention of asking them what they were carrying and where they were going. The men dropped their bags on seeing the Police and ran off with both policemen in hot pursuit. They split up and ran off in different directions, so the policemen split up and followed. Piet chased his man down a lane near some warehouses and on rounding a corner was grabbed by his suspect and another man who were overpowering him and trying to remove his revolver. The lanyard broke in the struggle leaving both men in possession of his weapon, so he had no choice but to run off at great speed before they decided to try and shoot him. He returned to the van at the same time as his colleague returned after losing his suspect.

They called for back-up on the radio and other vehicles came to the area to look for the suspects, but the area was becoming increasingly busy and the men could not be found. The goods that that the suspects had been carrying were examined and found to be items stolen from a residential housebreaking.

A few days later a report was received from a woman who had been robbed in her home in Umbilo. Gert Van Den Berg was the Umbilo Van Driver who attended to the report. The complainant reported that she opened her front door after a knock and before she could enquire who was there, two African men forced their way into the house and tied her to a chair. They gagged her and took their time in searching the house for choice items to steal. They took items of clothing and jewellery and packed them into suitcases found in the house and then left. The woman was able to free herself shortly thereafter and phoned the police. Gert circulated a description of the men, their clothing and the suitcases to Radio Control which was in turn passed onto other vehicles. Gert took a statement and got back into the vehicle to return to Umbilo to open a case when Control informed him that the Railway Police at the Berea Station had arrested two men in possession of suitcases with property that appeared to be stolen as they were unable to give a satisfactory explanation about the items.

Gert and his crew were despatched to the Berea Railway Station to pick up the men and goods. On his arrival he saw that the men and suitcases seemed to match the description given to him. The men were handcuffed, and Gert asked the Railway policemen to confirm that they had been searched and that other arrest procedures had been carried out. They confirmed that the men had been searched and cautioned. At the police van, Gert opened the rear and the Railway policeman removed his handcuffs as he was not going to accompany them to the Police Station. The two suspects climbed into the back of the van and Gert bent down to lift the suitcases into the van. As he looked up, he was staring up the barrel of a revolver in the hands of one of the criminals just as he fired. The bullet hit Gert just below his throat and travelled into his chest cavity just missing his heart. He fell to the ground in a serious condition as the men ran off down a little lane.

Several Squad Cars and Dog Handlers were despatched to the scene. Constable Johnny Aissing and patrol dog Charlie were first on the scene in minutes. He was shown the direction in which the men had fled so he took Charlie to see if he could pick up a spoor. Fortunately, there were few people around and since he was on the scene very quickly, Charlie picked up a scent and proceeded down the lane, which led to the rear of a block of flats. Charlie indicated the spoor continuing up fire escape stairs which Aissing, Charlie and other Dog Handlers ascended to the second floor roof top. Charlie was excited indicating that the scent was still fresh. He went to the corner of the roof top to a few plants in large pots, barking as he charged in and tackled the two men who had hidden themselves. They tried desperately to fight off the dog and escape but Aissing and his colleagues were mindful that they probably had a revolver so they climbed into them robustly to overpower them before a weapon could be used.

The men were taken into custody and searched. A member of the public in a nearby flat overlooking the rooftop where the action was taking place had seen the two men climb onto the roof and pointed out a place where she had seen them conceal something. The area near the pot plants was searched and the revolver was recovered. The revolver was found to have been issued to Piet Van Der Merwe, so the men were probably the same criminals who had overpowered him some days earlier.

Gert was taken to hospital in a critical condition and after a series of operations he began to recover slowly spending around eight weeks in hospital before being sent home to recuperate further.

The two men were charged with attempted murder and robbery and were sentenced to long terms of imprisonment. Due to the seriousness of the case and the good work done by Aissing and his dog, Charlie was awarded the Medal of Honour for Courage and Faithfulness. Gert kept the press clippings for many years as well as the bullet which was removed from his chest.

The story does not end there. In 1978 when I was Station Commander at the Somtseu Road Police Station, a colleague was checking fingerprint records that the Criminal Bureau had provided of a criminal arrested for theft. The record showed that the man had previously been convicted for attempted murder and robbery, and from the detail on the document we were able to confirm that this was the man who had shot Gert back in 1965. I had a copy made of the fingerprint record, which showed he also had a number of other convictions over the years. I gave it to Gert to add to his file on the shooting that almost cost him his life.

I realised within a few weeks that the policy of transfer on promotion was sound as it enabled one to start in a new environment with the authority and respect of the new position. I was quick to study the crime register to get a good understanding of local crime trends. Stamford Hill Police Station was a large converted house with 3 cells in the back yard, used mostly for arrests prior to appearance in court. A smaller house in the same grounds housed the Detective Branch as well as the Gold and Diamond Detective Branch which specialised in illegal dealing and thefts usually by highly sophisticated gangs with an overseas connection.

When I took over the Charge Office from the Sergeant who was going off duty, the primary responsibility was to check the cell register and then physically count the prisoners in the cells, to check the prisoners' receipts for property and fine and bail money. Shortages in any of these areas, and particularly missing prisoners, would lead to disciplinary action. I had heard stories where a prisoner had been irregularly released or had escaped and the new shift had not checked and signed a receipt for the missing prisoner. This had been discovered several hours later after hourly visits to cells had been recorded to reflect that a missing prisoner was still in custody. The negligence in accepting incorrect prisoners in detention and records could not be passed off as a harmless mistake. A policeman who messed up would get a reputation of being slap dash by policemen across the city.

We knew to be very careful when visiting the cells because prisoners may try to distract or attack you to make good an escape. One evening, Gert Van Den Berg was on duty and a commotion broke out in the cells. Gert and an African Constable ran to the cells and began to unlock the door. It sounded like a fight had broken out, but as Gert swung the door open, he saw a prisoner standing with the toilet bucket in his hands just as he threw the contents into his face. Gert was blinded by pee and poo. The prisoner tried to run past him, but Gert's bulk and presence pushed him back. The prisoner ran at him again to try to barge him out the way. Gert aimed a tremendous kick at him, missing the man but hitting the step at the cell door. The force of the kick broke Gert's boot and several of his toes. The African Constable used his baton to strike the prisoner on his arms and legs, and he finally retreated into the cell and gave up his escape attempt.

———

I was on duty in the Charge Office one evening around 10pm when a couple were brought to the station by friends to report the theft of their motor car. They had been at a wedding reception at the Saint Joseph Church Hall and had all come out to see the bride and groom leave. They then went back to the hall for a final drink and returned to where their car was parked only to find that it was gone. I took their particulars, registered a case of theft of motor car, and they left to go back to the hall. I contacted Radio Control and circulated the stolen car details.

A short while later the complainants returned to the station with a possible explanation for their missing vehicle. They owned an old early 1960's Morris Minor and so did the Groom. On their return to the hall they found that most of the guests had left and another Morris Minor was parked in the parking area some distance from where they left their vehicle. Their key would not open or start the other car, so they came to the conclusion that the newlywed couple had taken their car.

I established that the couple had gone to a hotel in town for the start of their honeymoon, so I phoned the reception and persuaded a reluctant hotel employee to put my call through to the Bridal suite. The groom answered the phone and thought that I was pulling his leg. I suggested that he look up the number of the Stamford Hill Charge Office in the phone book and phone immediately and as I would answer the phone and he would realise that it was not a prank. I could hear his new wife laughing in the background. He phoned back immediately, and I gave him the details of the two vehicles and requested him to go to the hotel car park to check the registration numbers. He phoned back a short while later and confirmed that he had the "stolen car". We arranged for someone to take the complainant to the hotel to recover their car and arrange a pick up for the newlywed couple the following morning.

My 1972 Chevrolet Kommando. A large number were used by the Dog Unit.

My father came to the Stamford Hill Station one day in February just before I finished my shift and suggested that we go to the Chevrolet Garage in Umgeni Road near the station, to look at the new Chevrolet Kommando. We test drove the new Chev which was a refinement of the Holden Premier that the Police Flying Squad used. It had a six-cylinder 4.1 litre engine with a tri-matic automatic gearbox. Dad suggested that I buy it as it offered a good discount. It was a great motor car and I had most of the money as I had been able to save money every month. I was frugal and had few expenses other than rent money to my mom. I decided to buy it for the R3500.00 price tag and made a large deposit and was able to drive off with my new car. My colleagues were really impressed with my new car. The price of petrol at that time still sticks in my mind. I could buy 3 gallons of petrol (nearly 14 litres) for one Rand (R1).

4

JOINING THE ELITE UNIT

I had applied to join the Dog Unit just before I left Umbilo and was advised that I was invited to an interview with the unit commander, Captain Hennie Meyer. Meyer and the Dog Unit both had an incredible reputation throughout police circles. I wanted to work with the best and because of my exposure to members of the Dog Unit, a number of them had recommended me to Meyer as a clever and fearless uniformed policeman. My interview was comfortable as Meyer had done his homework and had got feedback from his senior Dog Handlers about the respective merits of the various applicants. I was selected together with 5 other applicants and told that we would go to Dog School in Pretoria in late June 1972 for the 4 month training course. I was really pleased, and my parents were very happy for me as this was a reflection of me making an impact in a very tough world. Where was this immature schoolboy who felt bullied and insecure at a new school!

The Station Commander at Stamford Hill was genuinely sorry to see me go as he admitted that I was dependable and ensured a steady set of hands on the tiller. I was contacted again at that time by Police District Headquarters who advised me that they were to send me on counter insurgency duties to either South West Africa

Caprivi Strip or Rhodesia as a Sergeant was required from our area. They would have to assign another Sergeant from the District as I was going to Dog School.

The Durban class of 6 policemen duly reported at the Police Dog School to the West of Pretoria. Our Instructor, Sergeant Rheeder, was originally a Dog Handler from Cape Town and had trained a few courses before we were assigned to him. Our class was selected from around 20 applicants and comprised Sergeant Siegfried Marè, a married man in his late twenties who was stationed at Point and who had been in the police for around 10 years; Constable Eddie Dutton who was married, in his late twenties and who had worked in the Transkei before transferring to Radio Control in Durban; Constable Eivind Gjosund, a married man in his late twenties who was stationed at Bellair; Constable Gordon Roberts and Constable Martin Wessels who were in Police College the previous year and who were relatively inexperienced in practical police work.

The Police Dog School was very different to the College which was run on very disciplined lines due the large number of students under training. We had individual rooms with communal bathrooms at either end of a passage. There was another class of 6 Patrol Dog Handlers from Cape Town and a third class of 6 Tracker Dog Handlers under training. The trainees' dining facilities were very intimate, and one had a sense of being an individual rather than one of a large group. There was also a canteen which was open most evenings.

On our first day, we were addressed by the Brigadier in charge of the Dog School and then taken off to the kennels to look at Alsatians that had been donated by the public that would be available for us to select the dog we liked. This was an anxious morning as some of the dogs snarled at us and we did not know if we would be bitten on entering the kennel to place a choke chain around our selected dogs' neck. I took a good-looking dog out and when we all had dogs we walked about with them whilst Sergeant Rheeder cast a critical eye over them. My dog seemed very timid so after an hour, Rheeder suggested that I take another dog out the kennels.

I then looked at another dog and saw that the name "Bruno" was listed on the wire. I took him out and walked around with him. From then on Bruno and I became work colleagues, man and dog, in a remarkable relationship that lasted for almost 10 years. We owe it to the animal to commit to them for life, and once the relationship has developed it becomes incomparable. The unique bond becomes even more intense when you have trained your dog to become part of a crime busting team where you spend your entire working day together and may have to depend on one another for your life. This became even more extraordinary because Bruno had a soft nature and seemed to know when he was on or off duty. I would take him to our home in Cavell Place when I had days off and he would enjoy my mom fussing over him.

Training Bruno in Pretoria Dog School

Training a dog is based on repetition, building a relationship, and lots and lots of patience. We started by teaching the dog to walk in the heel position on the left side of the Handler. We were taught how to groom and feed the dog, and how to recognise various dog ailments and their treatment. We developed the dogs' confidence by taking them over obstacles, and walking over raised planks and through pipes. This would later be done on command and in the form of a drill. We began to teach the dogs to search for items strewn over an area of ground and then, as they became more proficient, over larger areas with undergrowth and bush. Items would include objects like pieces of cloth, screw drivers, knives, guns and bullets, as this would be typical of searching an area near a crime scene. This would be most useful after dark as the dogs' sense of smell would find these items when time was crucial to an investigation.

Tracking and following spoor (scent) became a daily practice with a dog school labourer walking through a section of bush or open veld over increasingly longer distances. He would then climb a tree and sit very quietly watching the dogs' progress. When the dog reached the tree, the labourer would tease the dog to get him to bark and indicate that he had tracked and found his quarry. The dogs would be taught to search an area of bush and buildings to find concealed persons and then indicate they had found them by barking. This technique was called "bark out". We would begin the tracking exercise first thing every morning and would travel to various locations to give the dogs a variety of terrain.

We would load the dogs into kennels on the specially converted truck and travel with the instructor and 2 trainees in the front with the other trainees on the back of the van. It was bitterly cold in Pretoria in the winter and we would shiver until we got to the tracking site. On one occasion we went past a fountain which was close to a tree. The strong wind had blown the spray from the fountain on to the tree which had frozen, decorating it with icicles.

We also trained the dog in aggression. Bruno was not a vicious dog and I had to really work on this area as he would bark and pull forward on a leash and grab the sack that was flicked at him, but it would be a different thing to attack without him feeling the security of being attached to me. A policeman would put on a padded suit and run, and the dog would be released after him. The dog was trained to go for the right arm and to grab hold until the handler came to release him. Most dogs may bite someone, but very few dogs will continue to attack or hang on to an item of clothing immobilising a person if that person is kicking or hitting out at them.

It was an interesting balance of getting the dog to be sufficiently aggressive to grab hold and to hang on to a suspect even if he tries to pull away and then to release on command and then sit whilst the Handler handcuffs the suspect. The dog will be inclined to fly into the suspect the moment the Handler touches him again. After much practice in college and for several months out on the streets, Bruno became very good in hanging onto the suspect until I commanded him to release and sit. He would then sit like an athlete in starting blocks waiting for the signal to attack again or react if the suspect tried to run away or attack me.

In the last week of the course we underwent a series of tests with dog and Handler being marked over the various exercises. All dogs passed the exercises as expected and we were issued with our certificates by the Brigadier. Arrangements were made to put the dogs on the train to Durban, but I opted to take Bruno home with me in my car.

My original plan of serving in the Police for four years to fulfil my National Service commitment was going out the window. I found the job challenging and fulfilling, and had been promoted at a young age and felt good about serving the public. I now had a dog which was a tool and a companion, and I was not going to walk away from that special relationship which strengthened with each case we worked on together.

———

The Dog Unit of the Flying Squad were the first responders who were always despatched to the most serious cases. Desperate criminals were often armed and would not think twice about injuring or killing a Police Officer. We were often despatched to serious crimes in progress such as housebreakings or robberies, as that type of criminal was more likely to run when we arrived on the scene. In some cases, the mere presence of the dog would make a criminal give up but when we surprised a suspect whilst attending a housebreaking or burglar alarm, they usually had identified at least two routes of escape and would take off like a turbo charged Jackrabbit.

When a suspect ran off, we would call on them to stop as we released the dog. If we spotted a suspect whilst driving the squad car, we had to develop a quick but slick routine that included stopping the car, putting it into Park, pulling up the handbrake, grabbing the torch next to you with the left hand, and removing the ignition key with the right hand as you opened your door, and then the kennel door to release the dog before you took off after the suspect at a sprint.

In most instances I would have a crew running after me as back up, but there were many instances when I was alone. The dog would usually run and grab the suspect by an arm and hold him until the Handler arrived. If the suspect continued to struggle or hit the dog, bite injuries were likely. In tackles where the suspect surrendered on being held by the dog, injuries may have only been scratches and sore muscles as the dog would often only hang on to clothing. Taking the dog off the tackle may not be the end of any danger. The suspect had to be searched for weapons and handcuffed.

As newly qualified Dog Handlers, we were allocated to one of four shifts. Each shift comprised about 10 Dog Handlers and a similar number of African Constables as crews. The dog cars or Flying Squad fleet comprised large fast cars mostly made up of Holden Premiers and Chrysler Valiants. There were still one or two V8 Ford Fairlanes and the Holden's were being replaced by Chev Kommando's. A car was usually allocated to 2 or 3 drivers on different shifts and a number of pool cars were available if your car was in the garage.

We were really fussy about the mechanical condition and

cleanliness of our vehicles. If a new Handler arrived at the Unit he would usually be allocated an older vehicle which he would share with another newcomer. It was rare for someone to have to speak to a colleague about the state of the vehicle, but newcomers were under no illusion about their obligations towards keeping their vehicles in good order. When we finished the shift, we were expected to fill the tank with petrol and hose out the kennel, so the new shift was ready to begin work immediately.

The Dog Unit headquarters and kennels were at Cato Manor Police Station which also housed single members in about 6 rooms. There was a large car park for about 20 squad cars and a prefabricated duty room which housed our lockers and had a desk for parades and meetings. The start of each shift began with a simple parade where everyone stood in 2 lines and were allocated vehicles, crew for the shift and the patrol area we were to cover. The shift leader was a Warrant Officer or senior Sergeant who would inspect the members for neatness and check our equipment which consisted of our revolver or pistol, extra ammunition, hand cuffs, large torch, 5 foot leash and a 30 foot puppy line for tracking. The shift comprised a number of Dog Handler Sergeants and Constables, and African Constables as crew.

The shift leader would read the information book and pass on any current information whilst the outgoing shift leader would give any relevant information that may have arisen during the previous shift. We would write up our pocketbooks which we kept open on a clipboard with foolscap paper for writing down complaint details or taking statements. We would then check our vehicles according to a predetermined check list that included head and tail lights, indicators and windscreen wipers.

We would book on the air with Radio Control giving our vehicle number and the names of the driver and crew, pick up our dog and then drive to our designated patrol area. Control would know when we were on the air and available for complaints, standing off at a complaint, back on the air from a complaint giving a short report so the complaint form could be written up and closed for filing. If we made an arrest then we would stand off at a station and report back on the air once all arrest documentation had been completed. The greater Durban area was broken up into regions with the majority assigned to Central, with others being assigned to Durban North, Durban South, Durban West and Outer West, so we would be available to back up the station vans and respond to serious cases in those areas. There was an "early car" which came on duty an hour earlier that the rest of the shift to provide cover for the changeover period when most cars and vans were at stations.

A large part of our work with the dogs was to respond to burglar alarms. Most commercial and industrial companies had fairly sophisticated alarms for the time. These would register an intrusion either by breaking the contact when a door or window was opened, or when an intruder walked through a beam, or activated a passive infra-red sensor. The alarm would be silently relayed to the alarm company who would either send an alarm technician to the premises or contact a manager from the company who held keys to provide access for a police search. I attended a great many false and positive alarms over the years and developed a great understanding of how Bruno's fine senses could read the situation.

When I received a report of an alarm at premises after dark, I would drive at speed, then slack off a short distance away and turn off the car lights. I would stop near the premises and approach on foot with Bruno to check the outside for signs of entry. The crew would usually go to the rear of the premises to look for signs of entry and to watch out for anyone escaping from the building. When the keyholder arrived, I would let Bruno smell him and he would then recognise him as one of the good guys. Any other scent in the premises found by Bruno would be recognised as an intruder. Bruno would search for a scent until he found a person hiding and bark to indicate his presence. If the suspect fled, he would then grab hold of the suspect until I reached him.

On arrival the keyholder would go to a control panel near the entrance to check which zone or area of the alarm had been triggered. False alarms could have been caused by poorly stacked goods that may have fallen, or the wind shaking contact alarms on windows. Poor maintenance or old systems often accounted for false alarms. On occasions, the control panel would be lit up in several demarcated zones in the premises which was a pretty positive sign of entry, but we had to establish if the burglars were still in the premises. I would ask the keyholder to accompany me to the area where the alarm had registered and let Bruno run off and search. Sometimes the scent was very strong, and I could see immediately by Bruno's behaviour that the burglars were either still there or they had just left the building.

One evening around midnight, I heard a colleague despatched to an alarm at the Eveready Batteries premises just off Umgeni Road near the bottom of Burman Bush. He reported that he was outside the premises, but he could not see any visible sign of entry as the building was surrounded by an 8-foot fence and the keyholder had not yet arrived at the scene. Sometime later I heard my colleague say on the radio that he was leaving since the keyholder had failed to arrive. Some 10 minutes later Control asked him to return as the keyholder had now arrived at the premises. He replied that he had left the area and was some distance away. I was not too far away and offered to attend.

On my arrival, I met the keyholder who had been there for a few minutes and was agitated as he spotted an open window that was closed when he left that afternoon. I shone my torch where he was pointing and saw faint shoe scuff marks on the wall below the window. Bruno and I accompanied the man to the door and checked the alarm control panel. We saw that 2 areas had been activated in the office part of the factory that was near the open window which had been forced open. I released Bruno who began to search from office to office. He was very active which indicated fresh scent.

He then went into a kitchen and was sniffing at a cupboard below a working surface. I was not sure if Bruno was distracted by the smell of food, disinfectants or burglar, so it crept quietly up to the cupboard door and jerked it open. In a split second I saw a burglar sitting hiding in the cupboard who was equally surprised to find a policeman and a dog looking at him. The burglar gave a loud shout which also surprised me, and I too shouted out. For a moment we were screaming at each other like frightened and surprised idiots. The keyholder turned and ran for the front door and I instinctively took a step back. It was a bit like a childhood nightmare of having someone unexpectedly step out of a cupboard shouting to frighten you.

Whilst we three humans were having similar reactions, Bruno was focused and jumped at the man with a growl, grabbing him on his arm and dragged him out onto the floor. I recovered my composure and grabbed the man, checking for weapons and took the dog off before handcuffing him. Bruno and I then searched the warehouse area but found no other presence. I took the suspect to the Stamford Hill Police Station, opened a case docket and left him in custody for the Detectives to follow up.

———

Despite the reality of crime and violence, the tight camaraderie amongst the members of the unit helped to maintain a sense of proportion so we did not let these burdens become too much. There were also moments of comedy which would be related by colleagues, often at the expense of their mates. Sergeant John Rabie was one of the older policemen who was a very neat man and was our units' version of "Cool Hand Luke". He did not wear his cap in the vehicle because it would mess up his hair. He would arrive at a complaint, get out of the vehicle and remove his comb from his long socks, run it through his hair before returning it to his sock, place his cap on his head, take a last drag on his cigarette before flicking it away as he walked with purpose towards the problem. John was involved in a funny incident which he kept to himself but it was inadvertently related by his wife to one of his colleagues and the story immediately went around the unit and raised a lot of laughs and sniggers.

John was patrolling in a suburban area one night when he spotted a suspect sneaking around an area of old houses, and derelict and recently demolished properties. The man spotted the police car, threw something away and ran off at high speed. John gave chase, and as he ran through this rough area, he suddenly felt the ground give way under him and he fell feet first into a hole. John found himself up to his neck in a septic sewerage tank. He made no report to Control about the incident, but placed as much paper as he could find on the driver's seat before driving home. His wife was woken by the sound of water spraying in the garden and looked out to see a totally naked John spraying himself and his clothing with the garden hose before he took a proper shower, got changed and then returned to work without a word to his colleagues.

When a new Dog Handler arrived from Dog School in Pretoria, the shift leader would usually put them in a car with an old hand for a few shifts to show them the ropes. When Constable Nickie Fourie arrived from Dog School he was posted as crew with John Rabie. Nickie had worked in Amanzimtoti to the South of Durban so he was a bit of an unknown with most of the members. One evening around midnight, John and Nickie were patrolling near the Butterworth Hotel which was a bit of a dive. In its better days, bands such as the Bats and Dickie Loader and the Blue Jeans played there. They saw 3 men brawling on the pavement. John stopped the car and they got out. Nickie later related that he jumped in between the men to stop the fight but they stopped fighting each other and focussed on him. He took several blows and then drew his baton which did not deter his assailants. He delivered a few well-placed blows to elbows and knees before they stopped fighting and surrendered to him.

He then looked to see what John Rabie was doing while he was mixing it up with the men. John was standing at the squad car with his one boot up on the bumper, an elbow on his knee whilst he casually drew on his cigarette. A police van arrived and took the men off to the Central Police Station. Nickie then turned to John and said that John should have helped him. John replied that he did not need to help as he could see that Nickie was handling the fight, and then suggested that next time he was engaged in a similar situation he should lead with his left hand, like a boxer, before striking with the baton in his right hand. Stories like that added to the reputation that John was one cool cop.

Some years later John transferred out of the Dog Unit and became a shift Indoor Supervisor at Radio Control where his great knowledge of Durban and crime was a terrific aid to develop the staff under him and support the Dog Unit in particular.

Dog Handlers were expected to keep a record of their arrests involving the dog, details of which were entered in a communal arrest register in the Dog Unit duty room. We all knew what arrests had been made and it created a level of healthy competition amongst the members. It became clear who the top 5 or 6 members amongst the over 40 dog handlers were and the desire to be the best was focussed on winning the Eric Gordon floating trophy for the most first schedule (serious crime) arrests in a year.

Eric Gordon, who had died some years previously, was the first vet who treated the police dogs. I was determined to do my best and after about 6 months I realised that I was as successful as previous winners of the trophy. When a serious crime in progress was reported to Radio Control, they would call, "Any vehicles in the vicinity of Main Road, Berea; housebreaking in progress." The cars would report their location and the closest cars would co-ordinate their arrival at the scene. More information would be coming from Control as we approached the address. The caller would be asked to remain on the phone and update what they saw including any description of the suspects or any vehicles that may be involved. In many instances, callers would stay on the line and report when the arrest was effected, or even add that a suspect may be hiding in a certain place, thereby assisting in their capture.

There was intense competition to get to the scene of a crime in progress because of the higher probability of making an arrest; however the overriding consideration was to catch the criminals and safeguard the public, so teamwork was essential.

I wanted to swing the odds more in my favour by knowing the entire Durban area suburbs and streets extremely well. I recall Control calling all dog vehicles in the area of road "X" as a housebreaking in progress was reported. Time was often spent with vehicles asking for directions to the address whilst I could use those minutes to speed along to the scene of the crime.

I would report that I was close and ask where the nearest other vehicle was to co-ordinate a silent approach to the address. Whilst there was a degree of healthy rivalry we operated as a team once we got to the crime scene. Experience of working together did not require much discussion. We would quickly agree who would take the back of the premises and the other members would automatically take the front to ensure capture and prevent suspects from escaping. We had confidence and trust in our abilities and in one another. We knew that when things got tough, our mates would be there, and we would not have to worry about going in alone.

5

CAR BREAKERS

I realised that you did not keep the city safe by waiting for cases to be reported. We had to find criminals either committing crime or leaving the scenes of crime ourselves. I would go to various police stations and chat with the Charge Office Sergeants to enquire about crime trends and where various types of crime were most prevalent. I would also read through the register of reported crime. Theft out of motor vehicles was a very prevalent crime which resulted in damage to the vehicle windows which were forced or broken, and damage to the dashboard area where radios and tape players were installed.

When I was not attending complaints in the early hours of the morning, the time that most of these crimes occurred, I would drive very slowly with the car's lights off along streets which were plagued by car breakers. I would stop the vehicle near an intersection and wait for 5 or 10 minutes to see if there was any movement. As the night shift approached 4 or 5 am, I would patrol along major transport routes as I realised that thieves would often lie low in parks or bush with their stolen goods until early commuters began to walk towards bus stops and train stations. They would then come out of their hiding places and mingle with commuters before taking a bus or walking towards their homes or criminal dens.

Car breakers were territorial by nature. They got to know an area with all the escape routes and back alleys. They would occasionally stay with a family member in the neighbourhood in which they operated, or they may have worked in the area previously. They would have their escape route planned and would often head towards major transit routes served by buses or trains.

Early one evening I received a report of a car breaker trying to open cars in the Berea area. The suspect was described as having a warm padded jacket which was unusual in Durban's climate. I spotted him by the description walking along the road and arrested him. He was in his late teens and when we searched him, we found him in possession of a screwdriver, some music tapes and some documents that appeared to have been taken from a cubby hole of a vehicle.

I took him to the Berea Police station where I greeted Constable Naude who was on duty in the Charge Office and began to process the documentation for the arrest. Naude caught sight of the warm jacket that the man was wearing and went to him, turning him around so he could look at a German flag on the sleeve. He said that he had a jacket just like that which was stolen out of his car some months earlier. He instructed the man to remove the jacket and looked inside the collar for a name tag. There he found a name tag with his name and address on it. Naude related that the jacket was not the sort that would be used in Durban's warm climate and that he had bought it about 2 years earlier to travel to Europe. The man now faced another charge.

———

At around 5am one morning I was patrolling my area when Control reported that a member of the public had phoned and reported that a man was breaking into cars and removing the radios in Oliver Lea Drive in Umbilo. Dog cars in the area were advised to proceed to Oliver Lea Drive. Control would then get back to the caller to get updated information to pass on to the police as they approached the scene.

In this instance I was some distance from the address and 2 or 3 colleagues were on the scene in a few minutes. By listening to the radio, I could hear that the suspect had fled the scene before they arrived, probably because they drove too close to the address rather than stopping some distance away and approaching on foot. I saw no point in driving past the scene or driving in the immediate area looking for someone who was now very alert to dog cars.

I put myself in the criminal's mind and thought that he could make two possible decisions; to lie low in the bush for several hours, or to move towards the main transport routes to mingle with commuters at a bus stop or train station. I felt that the second option would be the most likely. I knew that Prospect Road was a long road which lead away from the crime scene to the buses and trains in Umbilo Road so I went and parked the squad car in a lane looking on to Prospect Road with a view up the hill about a kilometre away from Oliver Lea Drive where the suspect had fled.

I placed myself between the area where the man had broken into the cars and the main road with access to buses and trains. I sat and watched the empty streets whilst my colleagues were racing around in the immediate area of the break-in. After about 10 minutes, I saw a man exit some bushes in a park walking at speed and looking over his shoulder in the direction of the crime scene. He did not see me as he was looking in the opposite direction. As he got to within 10 or 15 paces of the vehicle, I got out and called him.

I stood with my hand on the door catch of the dog kennel. I could see that his first thought of running for it was replaced by the thought of being caught by a large dog that was looking very attentively at him. He was sweating profusely which is often an indicator of stress. He gave himself up not risking it to attempt to outrun the dog. This was an example of the deterrent effect of the Dog Squad in effecting arrests.

I searched him and found a screwdriver in his pocket as well as a 2 or 3 radio switches. Car breakers would use a screwdriver to force a vent window to gain entry to the car and then remove the on/off and tuning switches to unscrew the radio from its fitting. I knew that I had found the man.

I took him to the scene and was able to match the switches to radios that had been removed from several cars. I knew that the suspect's fingerprints would probably be found on the side ventilation windows that he forced and the radios that he removed and hid in bushes near the scene. That would make the case against him almost watertight. I handed the suspect over to the Constable who was opening the case.

Dog Unit members got to know the hot spots for car breakers. Quiet tree lined streets were a favourite area to break into cars to steal car radios, tape decks and other valuables that may be left in the cars. The trees made the street lighting a little less effective and provided shadows to shelter the breakers as they went about their work. The off-road parking areas of blocks of flats also provided a good opportunity to break into several cars at one place.

Around 2.30 on a January morning in 1973, a resident in Flamingo Court noticed a man looking into a number of cars. He phoned Police Radio Control and reported his suspicion that the cars were being broken into. The front of Flamingo Court was in Umbilo Road with Gale Street running along the rear of the flats. I was about 5 minutes away and a colleague was also close so we agreed that I would approach from the Umbilo Road side and he would approach from the Gale Street side.

We stopped our vehicles a couple of hundred metres away and approached on foot with our dogs. As I entered the grounds of the flats, I got down on my haunches to look for signs of movement. I saw someone next to a vehicle and saw the interior light come on as the door opened. I moved closer very quietly keeping a low profile and I saw that Bruno had seen the man as well. There was suddenly a shout from the other side of the flats, and I saw two men run off in different directions with one coming in my direction.

I stood up and called on him to stop. He saw me and angled off away from me with no intention of stopping. I released Bruno who took off after him as I followed in close pursuit. I saw him drop something as Bruno grabbed hold of his arm and I then caught up and took him into custody. I looked in the area where he dropped an item and found a screwdriver. I heard more shouting at the other end of the flats car park and realised that my colleague had caught a second person.

We brought our two suspects together who were both young white men. We questioned the suspects and asked where they lived and after some evasion, we concluded from their accents that they were not Durban residents. We suspected that they must have a car somewhere. We brought the squad cars down into the car park and locked our suspects into the spare kennels. The squad cars had the rear seat removed and were fitted with two kennels with access via each of the rear doors. As we usually only had one dog per car, the second kennel was used to safely lock up any suspect as there was no door latch in the kennel, until you could take him to a Police Station. We then looked for a car that had a warm exhaust pipe or engine to identify what may have been the vehicle they were using.

The shouts had woken some of the residents and lights began to come on in the flats. Some residents came down and checked their cars for any damage. We identified around 8 cars that had been tampered with and had radios and other items removed. The residents identified a car that looked suspicious. We found a car key on one of the suspects that fitted the suspicious car's ignition, so we began a check of the contents. We discovered a stash of stolen radios and tape decks and found that they had also been siphoning petrol from some of the parked cars.

We took particulars of the vehicles that had been broken into and detained the suspects at the Umbilo Police Station. The overall value of the stolen radios may seem to be small, but it was big in relation to the salaries of the working class residents of the flats. Damage to the vent windows and damage to the dashboard in removing items or breaking of cubby hole locks added to the hassle in making good any loss.

6

AN UNLIKELY CRIMINAL

The Musgrave Road area on Durban's Berea was an upmarket area with large houses and well- to- do residents. One morning in 1975 two ladies were having tea on the verandah of their house when they saw a White Mercedes car draw up outside a house a few doors away. A middle aged, well-dressed White man got out and went into the property. He appeared to be looking around the property and left after about 30 minutes carrying a bag which he put his car.

The ladies felt that he was acting suspiciously, notwithstanding that he was well dressed and drove an upmarket car. They felt sufficiently uneasy to phone the police. Police Radio Control contacted Sergeant Vince Zimmerman of the Dog Unit to attend and he interviewed the two ladies on his arrival. The profile did not seem to reflect the type of person who would be up to no good but none the less he went to check to see if anything was out of the ordinary at the house in question.

In the early 1970s, most homes did not have high levels of security and access to properties would be through an unlocked pedestrian gate or driveway gate to a garage at the rear. The front fence or wall would usually be low and would not be a major barrier to entry. Zimmerman walked around the house and found the front door unlocked. There was no sign of forced entry. He looked around inside the house without conducting a thorough examination and things seemed to be in order, but his intuition told him that something was not right. He reported his findings to the ladies who had taken the registration number of the Mercedes.

At the time, vehicle registration for Durban vehicles with the distinctive ND plates was held at the Durban Council Licencing Department. Police Radio Control was asked to phone the Licencing Office to get the name and address of the registered owner of the Mercedes, and after some time these details were provided. As the Licencing Office worked regular office hours, Police had access to the records after hours by getting a key to the Licencing Offices from the Durban City Police Charge Office nearby and going through a card index.

Zimmerman went to look for the address that had been provided but realised that the address was either false or incorrectly registered. Police instinct kicked in and he felt that the suspect may have registered the car to a false address to cover his criminal activities.

The usual procedure at that stage would have been to contact the owners of the house, to confirm what was stolen and open a case whilst circulating details of the suspect and the vehicle with false plates and leave it to the Berea Police Station Detectives to investigate. Zimmerman was intrigued by this case as an unlikely suspect appeared to be going to great lengths to fit into an upmarket area and was covering his tracks with false number plates. He asked Radio Control to check their card index of stolen vehicles or vehicles that may be wanted in connection with a crime.

The Police Radio Control Indoor Supervisor went through the card index which held details of vehicle registrations in ascending order. He found no record amongst the index of stolen vehicles and decided to look at the index of closed cases or recovered vehicles. This was a long shot, but he found that the white Mercedes had been stolen some months previously, and had been recovered and handed back to the owner. The owners' details and address on the card were different to the record at the Licencing Office. This address was likely to be correct because the police would have wanted proof of identity before handing back a stolen vehicle to an owner.

Zimmerman decided to follow this up himself while the suspect may still have the bag with him, so he called for Constable Len Hutton of the Dog Unit to join him and they went to the address and looked for the white Mercedes. The car was not there so they posted a Constable near the address with a radio and he was to conceal himself nearby until he saw the car arrive, and report it. A short time later the Constable reported that the car had arrived. Zimmerman and Hutton went up to the flat on the top floor of a 3 or 4 story block after posting the Constable to watch the back of the property in case the suspect had a rear escape route.

They knocked on the door and they then heard a lot of scurrying around. They thought that the suspect was going to destroy or conceal valuable evidence so they tried the door, but it was locked and calls to the person inside got no response. Zimmerman held the door handle down in the open position and Hutton who was built like a rugby prop forward slammed into the door bursting the lock and the door flew open. They entered the flat with pistols drawn and immediately saw two persons pointing guns at them which gave them an adrenalin spike before they realised that they were looking at their reflections in a full-length mirror. They found the suspect as described by the witnesses who was very shaken and ill at ease.

Zimmerman asked the suspect why he had been at the address on the Berea earlier that day. The suspect replied that he worked at a local Estate Agency and he was looking at houses that were for sale as part of his job. They proceeded to search the flat and the car. The flat contained a quantity of silver cutlery sets including one that was still individually wrapped, as well as several calculators and cameras. A 16mm film projector caught the policemen's eye as an unusual item. The large number of items of the same type was suspicious, and the well-dressed man was asked to account for the items. He claimed that they belonged to his wife. Zimmerman asked for her phone number and contacted her in the presence of the suspect. She denied having anything to do with these items and said that her husband claimed to buy and sell at auctions.

Zimmerman also noticed a Hasselblad camera which was an expensive camera used by professional photographers. Zimmerman feigned interest in the camera and asked the suspect when and where he got the camera. He responded by saying that he bought it at an auction some months ago. He was then asked what photos he had taken, and he replied that had not taken any yet. It was abundantly clear that he was lying as you don't buy a specialist item for your hobby and not use it. Things were looking bleak for the suspect. He was seen carrying a bag when coming out of a house that had been broken into, his car had a false registered address, he was in possession of a large collection of valuable and saleable items, and his explanation for the items had been denied by his wife.

Things were about to get worse when Zimmerman found a list of house addresses in the suspects possession which he claimed were properties for sale in the area. The list had ticks against many of the addresses which Zimmerman checked against cases of housebreaking registered at the Berea Police Station and found many of the houses on his list had been broken into in recent months. He was ticking off the houses he had broken into. There were numerous house keys in bunches in the suspects case which he failed to account for.

The police were able to contact the owners of the house that the suspect had been seen entering that morning and they confirmed that they had recently bought the house and moved in. The house had been burgled shortly after they took occupation some weeks earlier with no visible signs of forced entry. They reported the loss of numerous household items including their entire silver cutlery set. Their insurance had paid out and they had replaced the items, so the cutlery still in the wrapping found at the suspects flat was their replacement for the earlier break in. Our greedy suspect had gone back to the same house twice.

Further investigation with the Berea Detectives tracked stolen items from other addresses and linked the dining room table and lounge carpet in the suspect's flat with break-ins in the area. The common denominator was that the victims had either put their homes up for sale or recently bought a home with the Agency for which the suspect worked. The Agency had obtained keys for homes so the Agents could take prospective clients to view the homes if owners were at work or away. It was found that the suspect had duplicate keys made so he could return to a house at a time of his choosing with a plausible reason for being there.

The suspect was charged with several counts of housebreaking and possession of stolen property. He was convicted in court some weeks later and received a ten-year custodial sentence.

Successful investigation of crime relies on the public noticing things that look out of order. This criminal had taken steps to blend into the area, but the tea ladies followed their instincts and took down the vehicle registration before calling the Police . An inquisitive and experienced policeman at the scene, and Radio Control going above and beyond the usual checks and procedures, combined to track down and take an unlikely criminal off the streets.

7

DAYTIME HOUSEBREAKER

One Saturday afternoon in October 1973, I received a report that a resident in Lanyon Grove, near the Botanic Gardens had noticed a young White male in the yard of their neighbour's property. The owners of the house were a young married couple who had gone away for the weekend. I drove to the scene and stopped 5 or 6 houses away from the place where the man had been spotted.

Warrant Officer Charles Chowles arrived as I was taking Bruno out of the car and we walked quietly up to the house. In most instances of housebreaking, a suspect will break in at a place that would be less visible from the street or neighbouring houses. The front of the house was visible from the street so it was probable that a housebreaker would have gained entry from the rear or side of the house. They would then usually open another door or window, so they had options to escape if the police arrived on the scene. The usual procedure for checking a potential break in would be to have one policeman take up position at the front whilst the other went around the house to check windows and the back door.

We carefully tried the front door handle, but it was locked.

Chowles then lifted the letter box flap in the front door and peered into the lounge. He spotted the suspect disconnecting and removing the Hi Fi set. For some silly reason he shouted at the man who immediately ran off to the rear of the house. Chowles shouted to me that the man was running out the back, so I ran around the right side of the house. I was already at a disadvantage because the suspect had a head start and as I did not want to slow up my dog Bruno, I released him.

As I got to the back of the house, I heard Chowles shout that the suspect was running down the other side of the house. Bruno ran past the open back door, immediately picked up the scent and ran off at top speed. By the time I got to the front garden I saw Bruno about to tackle the young White male suspect who had already reached the road and was running at his best 100 metres pace. Bruno brought him down, but he jumped to his feet and tried to get away from the dog's grip on his trousers. During the few seconds that it took me to get to him he sustained bite wounds on his leg that required a stitch and a tetanus injection at the hospital.

I locked him in the spare kennel in my car and went back to the house. I found two suitcases packed with various items of household goods ready for removal. The goods would be exhibits in the court case so I placed them in the car for removal to Berea Charge Office where they would be itemised for the case docket. I handed the suspect over to the Charge Office Sergeant and sat in a back room to write my statement and asked the Charge Office Constable to itemise the goods.

About 3 months later I was required to attend Regional Court. I checked the docket with the prosecutor before court started and saw that the young man already had a number of previous convictions for housebreaking. I was in the habit of going to the holding cells to look for my accused to make sure that I recognised him in the box. He immediately asked if the case was going to be withdrawn and if he would be let free. I asked him why he expected that to happen when he was caught red-handed. He said that he had found pornography and the complainants would not want that to come out in court. At that time, the South African laws were very strongly influenced by Afrikaans Calvinism and a case of possession of porn would have been eagerly followed by the media and a conviction would have had a social stigma.

I asked the accused "What porn?" He again said that he had found porn and put it in the suitcases. I told him that I did not know what he was talking about. He dropped his head and mumbled to himself.

I went to see the house owners who were waiting outside the court in the witness and public area. They had seen the list of items that had been packed for removal and were concerned about what was not listed amongst the goods for removal. They asked if certain magazines had been found in the cases. I replied that I did not know what they were talking about. I then told them that the accused had also asked about porn, but I told him that I did not know anything about it. They relaxed visibly.

The case proceeded very quickly as the accused plead guilty and the complainants were not required to give evidence. I gave my evidence but was not questioned about the items in the suitcases. The accused's attempt at a little extortion did not work. I think that it was quite probable that there was pornography in the suitcases, but I did not allow that allegation to cloud an open and shut case.

8

STRIKES; HURRY UP AND WAIT

There were widespread strikes in Durban during 1973, starting at the Corrobrick Brick works in North Coast Road and spreading to the textile industry. The magnitude of the problem stretched our resources, so we were placed on 12 hour shifts; a day shift and a night shift. All days off were cancelled for the foreseeable future. Strikes in the South African context were very different to most other parts of the world. The issue of race, politics and potential for violence was always a reality. The strikers would gather with sticks and knobkerries and intimidate and beat any African or Indian who attempted to report for work.

I decided to work on the night shift so I could focus on dealing with real crime rather than driving from one factory to another and sitting around for hours in case something happened. The strike petered out after about a month. The strikers gained some concessions for higher wages and Organised Business decided to redefine the industrial relations environment. Workers committees were established, and management met with staff representatives to provide a means of dealing with workers' issues.

Whilst many issues revolved around the workplace, training, advancement and wage matters, the socio-political problems were always just below the surface. Modern South African Industrial Relations evolved from the 1973 strikes. In later years, political observers stated that the African National Congress had not orchestrated the strikes and were initially unprepared to gain maximum mileage out of the events; but the power of the massed workers had been demonstrated and the labour movements would be the training ground for up and coming political activists.

A month or so after the strikes had settled, there was a strike at a Sugar Mill about 40 kilometres north of Durban. The local police attended the scene as well as a couple of Dog Unit personnel. The mill workers had basic skills whilst the cane cutters were very unsophisticated and gathered with their sticks and knobkerries. A scuffle broke out and some mill supervisors and staff were assaulted and threatened. Police reinforcements were called from Durban.

The Dog Unit Commander, Captain Hennie Meyer, brought 5 or 6 of the office staff up and the 3 or 4 Dog Handlers who were on duty, including myself, were sent up to the mill. At that time, the police did not have a dedicated riot or reaction unit. There was a police quartermaster store with some riot equipment which comprised long batons and Second World War helmets, but nothing like the equipment of modern riot units. There were no further incidents, but we remained outside the mill until about 6pm when most of the workers left to go home.

I did not enjoy sitting around waiting for things to happen. I am mildly hyperactive so I always looked for something to do, even if it was aggravating some of the more senior Afrikaans guys who called me "Engelsman". Some of them could not take a joke too well. Warrant Officer Fred Pautz was very fastidious about his van which he used exclusively for his dagga (cannabis) dog. I waited until he left his vehicle and then placed some orange peels and a banana peel on the floor. When he returned to his van he had a fit and said he knew that it was me.

The rest of the group were equally bored and were amused by Pautz's response. Flip Sonnekus went to Captain Meyer and proposed to set Fred Pautz up for another leg pull. Meyer went to

Pautz and said that some of us would remain at the mill whilst the rest of us took time out at the nearby Country Club. He then told Pautz to put his dogs into Flip Sonnekus' truck and give me his van to drive. Fred was in a rage but too disciplined to challenge the Captain. He came to me with the keys to his van and told me to "take the van and to f***" it up properly" so he could get a new one. After about 5 minutes Meyer told Pautz that it was a joke.

Sitting at a gate watching a group of strikers for hours on end was almost beyond my patience. I should have gone off duty at 2pm but it was decided that we should go to the nearby Country Club, have something to eat and stay over for the night in case further problems broke out. We fed our dogs and then went in for supper. The bar was full of local farmers who kept the bar counter in front of us lined up with beers. By 10pm we weaved our way to our rooms. I was to share a room with Constable Les Cregoe. Les was 2 or 3 years older than me and had worked in the Point area before joining the Dog Unit a year before me. He was the coach of a youth soccer team in Redhill and was very involved with the community. He passed the promotion exams to Sergeant in the late 1970's and took a posting to the Dog School in Pretoria as an Instructor.

I had no change of clothing, so decided to sleep naked. I placed my trousers on a chair near my bed and hung my tunic carefully over the back of the chair to look reasonably neat the following morning. I placed my shoes and socks under the chair.

I recall the Manager of the Country Club suggesting that if we went to the bathrooms down the open verandah then we should wear shoes as the mill deposited a light covering of dust and ash on the pathway. I got into bed feeling a little tipsy and put out the light. Les was in a worse condition than me because he said that the room was spinning. He suddenly jumped out of bed and dashed for the door, but he headed in the wrong direction falling over my chair. As I turned on the light I heard him throwing up, and saw him on his hands and knees over the fallen chair and my clothing. I grabbed him and pushed him out onto the lawn to finish puking.

I checked my clothing and found that he had barfed down the front of my tunic with a little on my trousers too. I washed the vomit off my clothing and reset my clothing over the chair to dry during the night. Les got back into bed and I went to sleep.

I woke up about 6am and was pleased to see that my tunic was dry. I picked up a towel and decided to take a shower. I put my bare feet into my shoes to walk to the bathroom but felt a wet, sticky mess inside my shoes as I stepped off with a squishing sound. Les had left a good deposit of vomit in both my shoes. The hazards of policing are not just limited to dangerous criminals, high speed car chases and attending to accidents when drivers don't slow down.

9

PATROLLING FOR HOUSEBREAKERS

Real police action happened on the night shift. We would report for duty at 9pm and work through to 7am. Friday and Saturday nights were very busy with a variety of complaints and we would no sooner finish with one complaint and report back on the air to Control, then we would get despatched to another. By 2am, the complaints had usually diminished, and we could meet a colleague at one of the few 24 hour coffee shops for a chat and something to drink. I would then go off to my assigned area and patrol along quiet suburban streets with my vehicle lights switched off, sometimes stopping near an intersection for 5 minutes to look and listen. Shortly after 4am, I would drive along the main bus routes into the city where I would look at the bus stops and train stations for criminals who would mix with early commuters as they made their way home with their loot.

At around 4.30 one summer morning shortly before dawn and as it was beginning to get light, I was patrolling without a crew near the intersection of Umgeni and Goble Roads. I saw a solitary man standing in a bus shelter with 2 large cardboard boxes next to him. I stopped the car, approached him and spoke to him in my very rudimentary Zulu. He began to reply in great detail so that I could not follow what he was saying. I asked him about his boxes which were tied and wrapped up in plastic.

I indicated that I wanted to see what was in his bundles, but he was discouraging me from doing so by his body language and tone of voice even though I could not follow what he was saying. He appeared to me to be a Zulu from the rural area as he had a knobkerrie, or a knobbed stick which can be used to very damaging effect. I considered calling for a colleague that had a Zulu crew to come and assist me in questioning the man, but I realised that most of the crews had gone off early to attend court.

I was considering leaving the man and driving off or risking a confrontation on slender grounds when I noticed something on the plastic shining in the street lighting. I shone my torch on the sheeting and saw a small trace of blood. The blood was on a place where the man had been holding and carrying the parcel. I instinctively knew that the blood was probably from a cut on his hand caused when breaking a window. I now wanted to open the parcel, but the man spoke in a very agitated manner and would not let me. He pulled the bundle away from me, so we stood there for a while having a tug of war over the object. He then raised his knobkerrie in a threatening manner indicating that he would strike me. I stood my ground and put my hand on my pistol holster then he began to walk away as I attempted to untie the bundle.

I called on him to stop and walked after him but he ran off at great speed into some bush nearby adjacent railway property. I ran back to the car and opened the door to release Bruno who had been sitting quietly watching the proceedings from the kennel. I also grabbed the microphone of the radio and blurted out, "Assistance required with arrest; Umgeni and Goble", and ran off in hot pursuit. Bruno had caught up with the man about 100 metres into the bush and I could hear the man swinging his knobkerrie and striking the dog.

I ran up to the man and grabbed the arm that held the weapon and began to wrestle with him. Bruno grabbed onto his trouser leg, but we could not overpower him between us. He was incredibly strong, and he was not going to give up or come quietly. Police dogs will become more aggressive with a person when their Handler is physically fighting with them and will begin to bite into a leg or arm with much more serious consequences. The pain will usually cause the person to give up the fight. Most fights or attempts to arrest a person, when a dog and Handler work in tandem, are of very short duration. The person is then usually subdued with bite wounds that require treatment.

We were involved in a desperate fight in a bush concealed from the road with an incredibly strong man who seemed oblivious to pain. This was a very unsavoury scenario. We would have to over power him, or he would seriously injure the dog and me and then leave the area. After about 2 or 3 minutes of struggling, I heard a rustling in the bush and suddenly another Alsatian launched itself into our adversary, shortly followed by my colleague, Sergeant Sparky Van Niekerk. Together we were finally able to subdue the man and handcuff him.

Sparky had arrived on the scene and found the car with the kennel door open but with no sign of Bruno or me. He released his dog, Duiwel (Devil), who quickly followed the scent and arrived at a crucial moment. We then opened one of the man's bundles and found several radios and electrical goods which appeared to have been taken from a store.

I took the prisoner to the charge office at Stamford Hill and began to open a docket for the offence of possession of suspected stolen property. I felt a great wave of weariness after my exertions and had difficulty holding my pen from the adrenalin rush. I sat still for about 15 minutes to let my sweating subside and to recover my composure. Sparky came into the station some time later and reported that Alan's Furnishers had been broken into and the owner was coming in to identify his goods. I thanked Sparky for backing me up. That was what we did, because our lives depended upon each other.

About a year after the fight with the strong man at the Umgeni and Goble Road intersection, I spotted another man sitting at the same bus stop at about 5 am. He too had a large parcel with him that was wrapped and tied up with a lot of plastic sheeting; the type of sheeting you find wrapped around boxes of new goods in retail shop's storerooms. He spotted the squad car as I was drawing to a stop near him and immediately ran off into the bush. I made the formal call on him to stop, but he was running as though he was going to break a cross country record. I released Bruno and my crew, Gcaba and I took off after him.

He ran through the bush, jumped a fence and crossed railway lines with Bruno narrowing the distance between them. As I got to the fence, a train came past and I had to wait for about half a minute before I could cross the tracks to support my dog. I could see them struggling in the flashes between the carriages. Bruno had tackled him, and he had fallen to the ground. His shoe had fallen off and he was whacking the dog with it. As soon as the train passed, I crossed over to where the man was trying to pull away, but Bruno had a good grip on his coat sleeve.

As I got to the man, he tried to throw a parcel the size of a half loaf of bread away. I grabbed him and handcuffed him. Gcaba joined us and recognised the man as a gangster from the African township of Kwa Mashu. I recovered the parcel and found it to contain cash in notes and coins; the typical contents of a shop cash register. We returned to the bus stop and opened the bundle to find that it contained clothing on hangers with the price tags still attached.

We took the man to the Stamford Hill Police Station and opened a docket for possessing suspected stolen property. We did not know where the goods had been stolen from at that time, but we knew that a shop owner in the area would come into the station in a few hours. The man started to bait Gcaba with insults and I could see that my crew was getting annoyed. I suggested that he ignore the man, but when he spat across at him Gcaba jumped up to assault him. I stopped him and pointed out that the man was going to go back to jail, and he was just trying to get Gcaba to strike him so he could lay a counter charge for assault and place Gcaba's job in jeopardy. A shop owner from Umgeni Road later identified his goods when he got to his store and found that it had been broken into.

We left him untouched and I was not surprised that when I went to court 3 or 4 months later, to have the man allege to the magistrate that I had allowed the dog to savage him for no reason and then punched and kicked him. I had relayed the events to the court in my evidence in chief and, under cross examination, told the magistrate how the man had tried to provoke Gcaba into hitting him.

The prosecutor asked the man if he reported the matter at the police station, in court at his first remand, or when he was remanded to gaol. His replies were unconvincing, and the magistrate found him guilty of the crime of housebreaking and dismissed his allegations of assault. The magistrate took the unusual step of stating in his finding that I was a regular witness in court and there had been no previous allegations of excessive force being used in arrests. He then related that I had been in his court a few weeks earlier in another case of housebreaking at an Antique Dealer's showroom where I had an opportunity to use my dog to find a suspect in the building but the suspect had given himself up when he heard the dog barking at the door he had smashed to gain entry, so I had not sent the dog into the shop to attack the man and he was not harmed in effecting the arrest.

———

Sunday morning shift was usually the most uneventful shift with very little happening until around lunch time when disturbance type complaints usually fuelled by alcohol started coming through. On a Sunday morning in 1973 I left Cato Manor kennels a little after 7am with Bruno and drove in the direction of the Berea. I was thinking about my uncle who lived in Florida Road and before long I was in Musgrave road approaching Mitchell Park and Florida Road.

Florida Road is a tree lined street that ran from Mitchell Park down towards the Greyville race Course with a mix of Victorian and Edwardian bungalows and double story homes. The houses were constructed of mixed material of brick, wood and iron with many houses having ornate cast iron work on pillars and balconies. Whilst some houses were a little run down, others had been well maintained and would have been very attractive to architects and the arty set. Many of the houses had gardens with lush shrubbery and palm trees that created a real colonial look.

I drove slowly down Florida Road looking at the houses with their large verandas and stain glass front doors when just ahead of me a man exited a front door heading for the front gate with two heavy suitcases in his arms. He clearly was not the owner or resident of the property and as we looked at each other there was instant recognition. He could see that I was a policeman and I could see that he was a criminal. He dropped the cases and ran down the road. I stopped the car and called on him to stop but he was running like his life depended on it. He had about a fifty metre start on me when I released Bruno who grabbed him by his arm and he gave up as I reached him.

I asked him why he ran and he did not answer. I then asked him what he was doing in the house I saw him exit and he denied he was there. I took him back to the house and saw that the lock of the front door had been forced. I left the man with my crew who put him in the spare kennel as I went inside. The house was upmarket and very tastefully furnished with fine carpets and fittings. The house had clear signs of disturbance. Lounge and dining room cupboards had been opened and items dumped on the floor. I could see that the cupboards and drawers in the bedroom had been opened with hangers lying on the floor. I quickly checked all the rooms and realised that there was no one else in the house.

I went into what would have been a bedroom on the ground floor which was fitted out as a second lounge with a wine rack across the entire side of the room. I had never seen a wine rack with so many bottles. Bottles were on the floor; some crudely opened with a lot sloshed on the floor. There were several boxes of matches on the floor with many used and burnt out. I surmised that someone was lighting dozens of matches to select a wine and it appeared as though many were not to the man's taste by the number of open bottles and mess on the floor.

I went into the kitchen and saw a frying pan on the stove which was still warm. The pan still had the remains of scrambled eggs whilst egg shells lay in the sink. The remainder of the contents of the egg tray had been smashed on the kitchen floor. I then began to examine the contents of the suitcases which comprised good quality men's suits, a portable radio and cash. I went back to the car and my crew told me that he and the man had been talking. The suspect said he broke into the house last night as he realised that the owners were away.

He was looking for valuables in the lounge and dining room before he found the wine room. He could not find a cork screw so he used a large knife to either try to dig out the cork or to smash the top of the bottle. He appeared to eventually have found something to his taste and after trying several other bottles by match light he fell asleep on the carpet. He woke up shortly after dawn and made himself something to eat before he looked for valuables to put into the suitcases he found in a bedroom. It was his bad luck that he timed his exit at the exact moment I was driving slowly by. This was not the first time that alcohol made a criminal forget his objective and it certainly will never be the last.

————

As a fit young policeman I did not have to release my dog on everyone who ran away if I could easily run after them myself and catch them if they were close to the car. The dog gave police a major edge as some criminals would not run if they saw a dog. Some criminals who did run at speed did not always continue to run straight down a road if they knew their crime scene territory. They knew the back alleys and which fences to jump to create obstacles for policeman and dog. The police dog increased the odds of catching a criminal before he ran into crowds or disappeared through other properties and found places to hide.

Whilst many criminals did not have an escape plan in the event of being stopped by the police a rare few were pretty clever. I can recall cases where a criminal jumped a fence into a property with a number of ferocious dogs and by the time he ran through and over the next fence, the dogs were alert when the policeman and his dog ran through and a dog fight ensued with the criminal making good his escape.

10

BURGLAR ALARMS AND DOG POOP

Burglar alarms were a constant in the life of the Dog Handlers. In the early 1970s there were only about three main companies that installed and monitored burglar alarms in premises, so Radio Control Indoor Staff got to know the Alarm Company controllers fairly well. Similarly, the Dog Handlers got to know the technicians who came out to sites rather well.

Alarms were installed to provide coverage of primarily business premises but there were a few domestic premises alarmed to protect the homes of the very well to do. The systems used comprised contact alarms on doors and windows that set off an alert when a door or window was opened. There were alarm beams that triggered when someone walked between two fixed points; usually down a passage and there were passive infrared movement detectors set up to cover an area that would register when someone moved into an area. These silent alarms were usually linked to an alarm company control room by a standard telephone line. As the alarms were silent, any housebreaker not familiar with relatively new technology may not have been aware that their break-in had been reported and that the police were going to check the premises.

When an alarm registered at the alarm company control room, the operator would phone the Police Radio Control and report an incident. The alarm company maintained a list of company keyholders from individual companies who would be phoned to meet the police on site and open the premises to allow a physical check with the dog. Some companies elected to have keys to their premises kept by a representative of the alarm company who would then meet the police on site rather than have their managers called out.

The dog handlers got to know which alarms were troublesome false alarms because the system was old or ineffective and those that were likely to be a positive intrusion. Alarms that activated in the middle of the night were likely to be positive but changes in weather such as thunder storms or high winds could set off sensitive systems. Alarms at night meant we could get there a lot quicker than dealing with busy traffic and we would stop a distance away from the address to conduct a quick external check before the keyholder or alarm representative arrived.

Bruno was a soft natured and intelligent dog who could instinctively distinguish the good guys from the bad guys. When the keyholder arrived, I would let Bruno smell him as he then recognised him as one of us. Keyholders were naturally nervous not only as there may be at a potential break in with what they saw as facing dangerous criminals, but there also correctly feared the dog. That was not a problem with Bruno and I would put keyholders at ease but there were some dogs that would want to bite anyone other than their handler once inside the premises.

Our usual procedure on arrival was for the keyholder to unlock the main entrance and go to the alarm control panel that was usually conveniently placed near the entry point. The alarm control panel was set up showing various sectors such as rear door, window contact points, first floor beams, or a passive infrared at a designated point. This was useful because we could isolate the problem to a particular part of a building, especially helpful when checking a large warehouse or multi story department store. On occasions when the control panel was opened we saw lots of lights indicating that access had been gained at several points across different types of systems. I often recall seeing a control panel opened looking like a Christmas tree and knew we had hit the jackpot; the only question then was whether the criminal was still in the premises or had made off quickly with some valuables.

After the parade at the start of a shift we'd receive important updates, our assigned patrol areas, and would collect our dogs from the kennels. Dogs are generally clean animals and only poop in their kennels if they had to. We would take our dogs out of the kennel and let them run in a caged exercise area to relieve themselves before we put them in the kennel in the squad car and set off to our patrol areas. We had a ten hour night shift and a seven hour morning and afternoon shift so making time to let the dog out to relieve himself and drink water during the shift was important. Sometimes things happened rapidly on busy shifts and the dog had to exercise control; but there were occasional accidents.

Many more English speakers were joining the Dog Unit when I came back from Dog School in 1972 so many of us newcomers were seen as a bit different by the older Afrikaans members of the unit. I was clearly a mischievous upstart but I was already a sergeant, could speak reasonable Afrikaans and was seen as a capable policeman, so the banter between the "Dutchman" and "Engelsman" existed as friendly rivalry.

One evening around midnight in 1972, I received an alarm at a large clothing store in Grey Street near the Mosque. I arrived within a few minutes and was joined by Sergeant "Ben" Schoeman. All Schoeman's at the time were called Ben after a former Minister of Transport named Ben Schoeman. Ben had been a detective at Umbilo when I arrived there as a student constable. His dog Nicky was donated by our neighbours in Manning Road because he would frequently jump the fence and bite pedestrians. In my last year at school, I left home on my bike and before I could build up some speed, Nicky cleared the fence and came after me. I tried to pedal faster to get away but Nicky caught me by my ankle and I came crashing down in the road. Nicky's owners called him back and as I was not hurt, I rode on to school but I had been taken down in a bicycle tackle which was a rare event.

The alarm company keyholder arrived at the clothing store after a few minutes and Bruno, Ben, the keyholder and I went into the store to check the control panel. A beam had triggered at the back of the store so I released Bruno with the instruction, "soek" or seek. We learnt to read our dogs at alarms. If there was fresh scent, the dog would become excited and we knew that someone had been in the shop. If the dog went off without a level of excitement, it would probably be a false alarm. We went to the rear of the store and found a cardboard box that appeared to have fallen into the path of a beam. We came to the conclusion that the box had been badly stacked on top of a pile of boxes and had fallen triggering the alarm.

I walked down a row of clothing racks towards the door when a smell hit my nostrils. There was Bruno with his back bent and raised as he pooped on the floor. I apologised to the keyholder, found an empty cardboard shirt box and with some dexterity was able to flip the poop into the box with the lid without leaving a deposit or smear on the carpet. I then went out into the street looking for a bin but there was none in sight however there was Ben's squad car. Ben never had a crew that night and as we switched off the interior lights of the car to conceal our arrival at crime scenes, I was able to put the box on the floor on the passenger side unnoticed and quietly close the door. Ben was chatting with the keyholder as I drove off and parked some distance away with my car lights off so I could observe.

I watched Ben return to his car and get into the driver's seat. I saw him get out and shine his torch in Nicky's kennel and then get back into the car. A few seconds later he got out again and used his torch to check his shoes. He then got back into the car and after switching his torch on together with the car's interior light I saw him open the passenger door and throw the box out. He then came onto the radio and said; "Engelsman; Jou bliksem!"

I felt that I had to brighten up a slow night shift.

———

Owners and managers of premises with alarms did not always take responsibility for their property and left it up to the Dog Handlers and alarm company representatives to sort out their problems when alarms were received. There were instances when the alarmed premises keyholder did not respond to phone calls and the alarm company never had a set of keys. The police would then be asked to make an external check of the premises which was not always adequate to report all clear.

On a Sunday afternoon shift in late April 1974, I heard Sergeant Boet Nel receive an alarm at SA Cargo Examiners and Repairers warehouse in South Beach Avenue just off Point Road. The area was a mix of warehouses, vehicle and boat repair garages with the occasional working class block of flats. On most Sunday's the area would be quiet with very little activity. I heard Sergeant Nel report that he was standing off at the address and he enquired if the keyholder would be arriving anytime soon. Control reported that the company representative was not answering his phone and the alarm company did not have keys to gain access.

As it was quiet and I was nearby, I drove up to the warehouse to chat with Nel. The warehouse was a relatively small single story building with another company workshop adjoining the right side and the rear of the property. The front of the warehouse had a vehicle roller door access that was secure and a front door with a frosted window nearby. The door and window were secure. The left side of the building had a vacant yard with painted out windows along the length of the side of the building. The windows were intact and Nel had already written up his pocket book to reflect that from an external inspection all appeared to be in order.

There was a large mangrove tree in the yard with a thick branch reaching over a section of the roof of the warehouse. As I am mildly hyperactive, I decided to climb the tree, move along the branch and get onto the roof. I thought that if I can climb onto the roof so too could a criminal. I climbed up the tree and onto the branch and to my surprise I saw a hole in the corrugated asbestos roof sheeting that was large enough for a person to climb through.

I called Nel up to have a look and he then asked Radio Control to get the alarm company representative to come out to the scene. When the representative arrived we decided to break the window near the front door and climb into the warehouse. I smashed the window with a baton and then opened the latch. I looked into the window and saw an office area with a door to the rear that was slightly ajar. I expected that the door would lead to the warehouse area. The window was a bit small so Bruno would fit through easily and I felt that I could squeeze through as I was a little trimer than Nel. I lifted Bruno up and he dropped into the front office area. I climbed into the window and was struggling to get my belt with the firearm holster through when I saw Bruno take off through the door leading to the warehouse. I dropped down into the office and unlocked the front door to let Nel in. We were looking around for an electrical panel to light up the warehouse when Bruno began to bark excitedly.

The warehouse was dark with very little light filtering in from the front office. I called to the alarm man asking him to find the lights as we went into the dark bumping into racks of pallets. We followed the sound of the barking and saw Bruno in the gloom barking at a figure on top of a pallet. I reached up to grab him and felt a slash across my right hand followed by the feeling of warm sticky blood flowing. I shouted to Nel, "He cut me!" Nel reached up and he too shouted out followed by a shot that flashed like lightning in the dark. Nel had shot at the figure on the pallet as I backed right off. I grabbed Bruno with my left hand and ran back to the office because I could feel my fingers had almost been severed. In the light of the office I saw a deep cut across from my little finger to the index finger with the bone exposed and the tendons cut.

Wounds to your extremities bleed profusely so I wrapped my hand tightly in a beach towel I saw on one of the desks but the blood continued to pour through the towel. The Alarm company inspector found the lights to the warehouse as another of our Dog

Handler colleagues arrived to help out. I was about to get into another dog car to be taken the two blocks to the Addington Hospital when they called out that Nel had a wound to his wrist and he had shot the man on the pallet. Addington Casualty section was quiet so I was taken right in for treatment. I had over twenty stitches to join my tendons and close the wound. I had a crazy thought that I may lose some fingers and had visions of going up to a barman asking for five beers whilst only holding up my thumb and pointing finger.

The Dog Unit Commander Major Hennie Meyer came into the hospital just before they finished sewing my hand to inform me that he had been to the warehouse. He reported that Nel was on his way to casualty for treatment and the suspect had been shot in the stomach and was also on his way to hospital. I was taken home and one of my colleagues put Bruno back into his kennel. My parents were concerned but did not make a fuss. I had some pain killers and went to bed. The following day, I was informed by colleagues that the burglar had died from his wound in hospital overnight.

I had reruns of the incident in my mind. What could we have done differently? Would it have better for me to climb through the window first and then ask Boet Nel to lift Bruno up to the window? That would not have worked because Bruno could have bitten him with the lifting and trying to push him through the window. We did not know if we could open the front door or not from the inside. I concluded that the issue was not having the keyholder to open the premises and put on the lights. A series of unfortunate events and a man had lost his life. I suppose that I was lucky as our injuries could have been worse but I had a great sense of regret. We had to get on with it and deal with it. Whilst Hennie Meyer was a commander who watched out for his men we got on without counselling because it was after all the 1970s.

I was off sick for around three weeks and was itching to get back to work as was Bruno. I would visit Bruno in kennels over this period but when he saw me in uniform for the first time he was so excited to get back in the squad car that he jumped up knocking my hand and causing the wound to bleed again.

An inquest into the incident was held in April 1975 where Magistrate PU De Jager found after reviewing all the evidence that the man, who had several convictions for housebreaking, was shot dead in self-defence.

———

Durban in the summer is usually hot and humid and any physical exertion causes a person to sweat profusely. One extra hot summer's day on a weekend in 1974 I received a report of a burglar alarm at a private house on the Bluff. The Bluff was a mostly working class suburb but there were a number of large houses built along the top of the ridge with views out to sea. These were the homes of the rich and affluent. In those days burglar alarms at private residences were rare and were intended to protect high value household items. I was informed that the alarm company reported that the owners of the property were away on holiday so I would have to conduct an external check only.

My crew and I parked some distance away and together with Bruno, walked towards the house. We entered the yard through an unlocked gate and I told the crew to take up a concealed position watching the front of the house whilst I went around the back. As I walked around the back of the house I saw a small window was open. This was a toilet window that appeared to have been forced. I looked through the window and saw dirty footmarks on the toilet seat. I told Bruno to "sit and stay" as I quietly sneaked around to the front of the house to tell the crew what I found. The crew would remain concealed and watch the front in case anyone ran out as I tried to climb in from the back.

I lifted Bruno through the toilet window and climbed through quickly after him. Once inside I sent Bruno off with the command, "Soek" as I followed quietly behind him. I could see from Bruno's behaviour that a scent was strong as body odour on a hot day was easy to follow. Bruno went into the bedrooms but very quickly came out and then went into the lounge where he darted behind the couch with a growl. He had grabbed onto a man who quickly stood up as I approached. The man put up a brief struggle before I handcuffed him and took Bruno off him. I made the man lie down on the carpet as I sent Bruno off to check the rest of the house for any other burglars. I waved at my crew through the window and indicated that I had arrested a suspect.

I checked the bedrooms and the rest of the house and saw that valuable items had been packed for removal. By that time, the burglar and I were like sweat balls of perspiration. My uniform felt greasy as I looked for a way out the house. I could not find any keys to open a door so I took the burglar back to the toilet window to climb out to my crew. I lifted Bruno up to the window and followed him out. We took the suspect to the King's Rest Police Station and detained him whilst I wrote out my statement for the detectives.

Some months later I received a witness subpoena to attend court for this arrest. I met the owner of the house in the witness seating area of the court and he thanked me for my actions. He then asked me if my dog had pooped inside his house. I told him that I didn't know as I had my hands full with the suspect and was looking for any accomplices that may also be in the house. He told me that when he got home two days later he opened the front door and the hot smell of two day old poop hit him. He found the poop on the bedroom carpet and wondered if it was my police dog or if the suspect had left it.

When you have your hands full at a crime scene you do not always have the time to do the housekeeping.

———

On a weekday morning shift in 1974 I was patrolling in Morningside which was an affluent suburb rising up to the ridge with sea views. Many of the houses were large double story houses many of which could be called mansions with multiple bedrooms, swimming pools and cottage type outhouses. These were the homes of successful business people and company executives. It was around 1.30pm and as shift changeover was at 2.00pm, I was going to drive up along Ridge Road and head back to the Dog Unit offices and kennels at Cato Manor. I was alone in the car as my crew was giving evidence in court. I heard Radio Control ask if anyone was in the Morningside area as they had an alarm at a residential property. I offered to attend and asked if any other vehicles were close as I was alone. Control said that most vehicles were standing off for shift change but they would see if they could find back-up.

They provided an address near the Arch-Bishop's residence and King's House which was the Durban residence for the State President so I knew what sort of house I was going to. I stopped a few doors away from the address and took Bruno out the kennel on his leash. The house was on a slope with a walk down a drive-way. It was a large extended mansion with garages to the rear. I was only a few steps down the driveway when I noticed a kitchen door was open on the side of the house. At that moment a man put his head out the door and saw me. He took off like a flash running down the driveway at speed. I released Bruno who closed the distance quickly as the man was about to reach the back end of the property. I hoped that Bruno would get to him before he reached a fence because if he cleared that, it would present problems following and leaping into the unknown.

The man was about to jump up the back fence when Bruno caught him by an ankle and he crashed face first into the fence. I was onto him before he could recover and handcuffed him. I expected that the man was probably not alone and I wanted to get into the house with Bruno and look for any accomplices, but what to do with the suspect? I ran him up the driveway towards the squad car. I was going to shut him in the spare kennel which did not have handles on the inside. The only way he was going to get out was if someone opened the door. I was worried if I left him in the car, a passer-by or an accomplice may release him.

As I got to the car, I saw an older bearded man walking up the road and recognised him as Fluffy Alexander, a geography teacher from Glenwood High School. I put my prisoner in the kennel and said assertively to Fluffy, "Guard him. I will be back". I ran back to the house and went through the kitchen with Bruno. Bruno picked up scent and ran through the house following his nose but I soon realised by his body language that there was probably no one else in the house. The lounge and dining room appeared to have been disrupted by the man's search and Bruno did not react to anything upstairs and in the bedrooms.

I went back to the car to find that Fluffy was dutifully standing at the door with the suspect pleading with him to open the door. I thanked Fluffy for helping me but I did not have time to introduce myself. He had not been one of my teachers when I was in school but he probably would not have known me. I thought that this was ironic because only 6 years earlier Fluffy could have been telling me what to do and now I was instructing him. I took the suspect to Stamford Hill Police Station and detained him for Housebreaking with intent to steal and theft; residential premises.

In 1975, Dog Handlers Pieter Du Plooy and Mervin Van Rensburg were requested by Radio Control to attend an alarm at a clothing warehouse in Umbilo a little after midnight. They were requested to do an "external" as the alarm company could not locate a representative of the company with a key to give them access for a proper search with a dog. They walked around the building checking doors and windows with their torches and noticed a fanlight window that was open and was large enough for a person to get in. On looking at the dust around the window it appeared to have been recently opened after a long period of being closed. They suspected that the window had been forced and entry gained. It was too high to attempt to push a dog through so they decided to conduct a physical search without the dogs.

Looking back and trying to contextualise this in modern times, it is hard to imagine policemen today going to that length to check out a potential break in when the owner cannot be traced. This is another example of how the Dog Handlers in the 1970s were not going to let a criminal get away if they thought outside the box.

They lifted one another and wriggled through the window with some difficulty and started to walk through the rows of dresses, jackets and other items of clothing. The policemen were walking along either side of a long rack when Du Plooy spotted something which may have been a person hiding amongst the clothing. Without saying a word he dipped his eyes and indicated the spot to Van Rensburg who nodded in response. Policemen working together at a crime scene knew one another well and knew what drills to follow, so there was little need to have a discussion about what each policemen would do. Van Rensburg was feeling in a mischievous mood, so he stepped back and aimed a kick in the direction of the clothing fully expecting to see a housebreaker propelled out the other side.

He had not taken care to check the construction of the racks which had a solid metal bar running horizontally along the base of the rack to help stabilise the weight of clothing. Van Rensburg's shin bone connected solidly with the bar. He later related to me that the shock and pain was numbing as he sank to his knees. At that moment the housebreaker's head emerged from amongst the clothing and said, "Sorry boss!" Van Rensburg said that he was speechless from pain and surprise and it took him some time to get to his feet. The housebreaker was taken into custody and Van Rensburg limped off back to his car. He limped for several days and had a bruise the size of his fist across his shin.

Lifting a dog to put him through a high window or over a high fence is a difficult task. Not all dogs liked the idea of being lifted and pushed through a small window with a drop on the other side and some would baulk at going through. One of my colleagues attended a potential housebreaking and found a small window open at shoulder height. He lifted his dog and positioned him so the dog could put his head and paws on the bottom of the window ledge. Instead of the dog climbing or jumping through, he used his front paws to block his body going through. The handler encouraged the dog and pushed him from the rear but the dog was not having it. The Dog Handler was a little annoyed as others were present so he gave the dog an extra hard push which caused the dog to poop down the front of his tunic.

That was it; game over. Another dog was called for to enter through the window. There is truth in the song, "A policeman's lot is not a happy one."

11

DANGEROUS DOMESTIC DISTURBANCES

The Police attend a fair number of domestic disturbance complaints, usually on a weekend and mostly with neighbours complaining about loud music or noise late at night. Some disturbances were not easily resolved and there were instances where drunkenness, drug use or mental instability made a disturbance complaint a lottery.

Rossburgh and Seaview in the early 1970s were working class residential areas and a part of old Durban where many of the older houses built in the early 1900s had tin roofs with colonial veranda's running around 3 sides of the house. Many homes had seen better days and needed repair whilst more modern small flats provided housing for "just getting by families". Constable Morty was stationed at Rossburgh and attended an incident where he stopped a person acting suspiciously and was stabbed in the cheek with a bayonet the man was carrying concealed in his trousers. The wound had healed but he was naturally nervous when a few weeks later he was asked to attend a disturbance complaint at a house in Railway Road where a number of previous complaints of the husband assaulting his wife had been received. He asked

Radio Control to send another policeman to accompany him to the complaint.

Sergeant Vince Zimmerman was directed to attend and on his arrival he was met by Morty who briefed him on the problem. They decided that unless the husband was calm and agreed to behave, they would arrest him and take him to the police station. As the policemen approached the house, the husband came out with his shirt off and he looked like a real tough guy. He was immediately aggressive and dismissive of the police. Zimmerman decided to arrest the man. As he turned to walk back into the house Zimmerman jumped on him in an attempt to bring him down, but the man walked into the house with Zimmerman on his back, then he threw him off and lay down on the couch.

The wife then entered the lounge wearing a nightgown and began to shout at the policemen. Zimmerman and Morty attempted to arrest the husband and whilst they were struggling with him, the woman's mother entered the room and attacked Morty. Morty grabbed the mother and locked her in a bedroom whilst Zimmerman continued to struggle with the husband. The wife then picked up a pot plant in a clay pot that was on a shelf, and smashed it on Zimmerman's head. Zimmerman was temporarily stunned but continued to struggle with the man as he felt the potting soil run down his back inside his tunic.

Whilst the two policemen struggled with the strong man, the wife went into the kitchen and took a heavy glass water jug and smashed it against the sink leaving the handle with jagged pieces of glass as a weapon in her hands. She approached Zimmerman from the rear and smashed him on the back of his head causing deep lacerations. The policemen now grabbed the woman to arrest her and in the struggle her night dress was torn exposing her breasts which did nothing to diminish the fight in her or the determination of the policemen to arrest them both. The husband then picked up a heavy coffee table to use as a weapon. At that stage Zimmerman drew his 38 revolver and told the man that he would shoot him if he persisted.

The sight of the revolver had the desired effect and the man allowed himself to be led to the van and locked in the rear. The wife was put in the back of the van with him and handed a blanket so she could cover herself. Zimmerman took off his tunic as the blood was flowing freely down his back. This decision was made to save damage to his tunic because policemen had to pay for and maintain their uniforms at that time. As Zimmerman was bleeding profusely and needed urgent medical treatment, it was decided to drive directly to the hospital with the husband and wife still in the rear of the van. On route to the hospital, the man became violent again and punched the window that separated the back of the van and the cab where the driver and crew sat. The shattered glass hit Zimmerman causing cuts on his back. Zimmerman was treated at hospital, receiving 19 stitches and a period of sick leave before he returned to work. The husband had broken his hand and the wife had some minor injuries that were also treated.

Things were calmer when they got to the police station as there were several other policemen to call on if the man became violent. The couple was detained overnight to appear in court the following day.

They were both charged with disturbance, resisting arrest, and assault on police. Some weeks later the wife received a prison sentence of 4 weeks and the husband received 2 weeks. This incident reinforced the view amongst policemen never to underestimate a disturbance complaint, to be prepared for anything, and never to let your guard down. There are some crazy people out there.

———

Durban's Point Road ran from West Street towards the harbour mouth and had a reputation as a red light district; but it was more than that. The part of Point Road closest to West Street had numerous holiday and residential flats, and the further one went down towards the harbour the less affluent and seedier it became. The area closest to the harbour had a mix of warehouses and businesses associated with shipping as well as night clubs that attracted local residents and visiting seaman, with the promise of good food, alcohol and ladies of the night, some of whom became more attractive with each drink consumed.

Durban's harbour was booming in the early 1970's as many larger tankers used the Cape route from Asia to Europe and the America's. The Arab States and Israeli wars of 1967 and 1973 made Durban a better route than going through the Suez Canal. Cargo ships, tankers and cruise ships used Durban and on any given day there would be in the region of 20 ships visible off the coast waiting to get a berth in the docks.

Railway trucks in the harbour worked 24 hours a day loading and off-loading cargo. The Union Castle line and Safmarine ships carried mail and passengers to Southampton. All these activities made the port an important engine of Durban and South Africa's economy. Many of the seamen were only in port for a day or two and after weeks at sea they were looking for places of entertainment and pleasure. Point Road provided what many of them wanted.

There were small flats above some of the businesses' and Polly's Lodge was a four-story building in need of renovation that provided rented accommodation for poor older people, and young families. The ground floor had a night club that stayed open until around three or four o'clock in the morning. Ladies stood outside the club enticing people to come in or drive off with them, and taxis came and went throughout the night. A little further down Point Road closer to the harbour entrance was the Alexandra Hotel which had seen better days and housed the Smugglers' Inn night club (Smuggies) which was a Durban legend. Strip shows and good food drew in many affluent Durban residents who were intent on a good night out and a look at another side of Durban that was not on the usual tourist itinerary.

Point Road was only two blocks back from the Durban beachfront (the Golden Mile) and comprised a mix of hotels from the upmarket to budget hotels as well as holiday and residential flats. The Snell Parade ran along the beachfront from West Street to

Bell Street with vacant land and a parking lot beyond, towards the harbour entrance. The beachfront was known as the Golden Mile and was a magnet to holiday makers from the Transvaal. Whilst close in distance, the Golden Mile and Point Road were worlds apart for the people who lived, worked and visited.

I received a complaint one Sunday afternoon in February 1973 to attend to a disturbance and assault incident at Polly's Lodge. February was a hot and humid month and I expected the complaint to be fuelled by alcohol. On my arrival I was met by a group of people who reported that a young male resident was having a heated argument with his pregnant wife and when neighbours asked him to quieten down, he had assaulted two of them.

I followed the two complainants who wanted to press charges and to see the man removed from the premises as he was drunk and abusive. We climbed the stairs to the third floor and approached a room. A young man came out wearing only a pair of shorts. He was identified as the assailant, so I told him that he had been pointed out as having assaulted two of his neighbours. I could see that he was moderately drunk and aggressive. I took him into his room and saw that his wife had a swollen face and she asked me to take him away.

I told the man that I was arresting him and to put a shirt and shoes on. He went to a cupboard and then suddenly jumped out the large open sash window. I looked down to see where he had fallen and saw a corrugated asbestos roof below the window, with a hole where he had fallen. The hole was almost in the shape of a person with a large shape for the body and broken parts where his legs and arms had smashed through the roof. A silly thought entered my head that it looked like a Daffy Duck cartoon when they show a body imprint as they smash through a wall or a roof.

I ran downstairs to the night club and to the toilets at the rear and found him lying moaning in a toilet cubicle. He had gone through the asbestos roof and the ceiling panelling that would have slowed down his impact with the tiled toilet floor. He did not appear to have broken an arm or a leg and was holding his stomach. I called Radio Control to get an ambulance which arrived promptly and took him to Addington Hospital a few blocks away on the Snell Parade. I arranged for the assault complainants to go to the Point Police Station to open a case of common assault.

The man was lucky that his intoxicated state probably contributed to his less serious injuries than one would have expected from someone falling from the third storey of a building. This was another sad example of people trapped in a cycle of poverty aided by alcohol, poor education and domestic violence. I reported the outcome to Control and waited for the next complaint.

————

One early evening in March 1973 I received a report of a fire at Keeler Lodge just off Point Road. Police were contacted by the Fire Brigade for all fire incident call outs as there may be cases of arson, a need to help evacuate a building or control a crowd. I approached the Fire Station Officer on my arrival as they were loading hoses back onto their machine. He reported that a fire had been deliberately started using petrol, but a resident had taken quick action and used an extinguisher to put it out before too much damage had occurred.

Keeler Lodge was a working-class boarding house where many residents were long term occupiers and knew one another. The Supervisor approached me to report that she and other residents were on the verandah having a drink. Another resident had been with them and became argumentative, so they told him to go away. A short time later they could smell petrol and thought initially that it was coming from a nearby parking garage. They followed the burning smell which came from the lounge. There they saw the man who had been arguing with them standing with a petrol container and a fire burning the carpeted floor.

One of the residents took a fire extinguisher and put the fire out whilst the Supervisor phoned the Fire Brigade. They told me that the man had gone to his room and was expected to be aggressive. At that moment, I saw the Fire Engine backing out of Keeler

Lane and recognised Willie Olivier on the rear of the machine. Willie was a Fireman and the South African Middleweight Wresting Champion, and I thought that as I was without a crew, having Willie close by when I confronted the aggressive man could be helpful.

It was my job to confront the man and I had to decide whether to call for back up without knowing how the suspect would respond or go in alone to take charge of the situation. The Supervisor took me to the suspects' room, and I told him what had been reported and that I was going to arrest him and take him to Point Police Station. He walked up to me and told me that he was not going anywhere. Experiences of similar incidents means that you do not back off but also do not adopt a threatening stance. I calmly told him that he had to accompany me, and we could sort it out at the station.

The suspect was in his mid-forties and a little bit bigger than me. I knew that many of the residents of the boarding house were pretty rough working class people often had a history of fighting and being able to handle themselves. He put his fists up in a fighting pose and advanced towards me. He threw a punch that I blocked and told him in a calm manner to stop it and come with me. It had no effect and he moved towards me again at which point the Supervisor ran off.

Being alone with a suspect you want to arrest when a fight seems likely is not ideal not only because a policeman may get hurt but it could be alleged that excessive force was used on a suspect.

I thought that the Supervisor may have gone to get help. My other option of going to the squad car to ask for back-up on the radio was not on because the suspect might run off or go after the Supervisor and other residents who informed on him.

The man threw another punch at me that glanced across my shoulder as I weaved away. I grabbed him around his chest and tried to pin his arms. He tried to throw more punches at me but by being up close, I was shutting down a punching fight. We got into a full on rough and tumble until I was able to pin an arm behind his back and force him to the floor. The pressure on his arm made him give up as I put the cuffs on. I took him to the car and detained him at Point for arson and resisting arrest.

In the early 1970s, the Police were unable to get radios that could be taken out of the vehicle and carried into a complaint or crime scene. If a colleague was sent to a disturbance and seemed to be off the air for a while, we would usually drive by to check if they needed any help. It was our way of supporting a fellow team member.

With advancements in later years a policeman could keep a radio in hand to update Radio Control or call for back-up which proved to be more efficient and resulted in fewer injuries to the Police and the public.

———

Not all cases were resolved following the book. Domestic complaints had so many individual issues that it would be impossible to write a manual on how to resolve them.

Late one midweek afternoon in 1976, one of my colleagues went to a domestic complaint in a block of flats in Aliwal Street opposite the City Hall. He went up to the fifth floor and was met by a woman who had phoned the police. The flat had a small balcony and he saw there was a man who had climbed over the balcony with a foothold on the outer edge and was holding on to the railing, with the pavement way down below.

The woman related that she and the man had been lovers, but his behaviour had caused problems and she had ended the relationship. The man did not accept this and had continued to pester her to take him back. The police had apparently been called to the flat on multiple occasions when he had pestered the woman to let him in. On a recent incident, the man had been told by the police that he would be arrested if he called again. On the day of this incident the man had knocked on the woman's door and had asked to be let in to talk with her. He promised that if she let him in to get things off his chest, he would never bother her again. The woman let him in, but he ran to the balcony, climbed over the railings and told her that he would commit suicide if she did not take him back.

The Constable went to the man to get his side of the story. The man was emotional and told the policeman to keep his distance or he would let go and drop. The Constable listened to him and applied reason and logic and told the man that his behaviour was wrong. The conversation went on to no avail for over an hour with a mix of empathy and pointing out that he was trespassing. The Constable asked the man if he had family who could be contacted to come and talk with him. Was he religious and did he want a minister or priest? It was now after 8 pm and as the Constable had a radio on his person, one of his colleagues asked if he was going to be at the complaint much longer.

Shift change was coming up and if the Constable did not get back in time to get the minibus home with the rest of his shift, he would have to wait for someone from the nightshift to give him a lift. That would mean getting home well after 10pm. The Constable was getting exasperated with the man because he could see that this situation was not going anywhere. He contacted Radio Control and asked for the Durban Central van driver to join him at the complaint. Once the Central policeman joined him, he got a bit more forceful with the man. He pointed out that the man was unreasonable, and that he would arrest him for trespassing. The man told him not to come any closer. The Constable told him that he had run out of patience and the man should either come in or jump.

The man complained that the Constable could not do that, and it was not fair to him. The Constable drew his baton and approached the man telling him to get in or he would throw him off. The man protested saying "You can't do that!" The Constable then began to hit the railing with his baton close to the man's hands saying, "You get in now or you can drop!" The man screamed, "You are trying to kill me" and climbed back onto the balcony where the two policemen grabbed him and handcuffed him. My Dog Handler colleague handed the man over to the policeman from Central so he could be charged and detained for trespass. He headed back to his squad car at speed whilst contacting his colleagues on the radio telling them to hold the minibus as he was on his way.

Not a textbook method but effective in this case. It could have had another outcome with the man plunging to the pavement. Situations such as this depend on the policeman's ability to read people and their state of mind to make a judgement call. In today's world this would have been a major breach of police duty of care, but it was the 1970s and things were different then.

12

HAIR RAISING CAR CHASE

Police instinct or gut instinct is something that a policeman develops over time and is the sum of his experiences where human behaviour and body language combine to give a predictive ability as to what may happen next, or whether a person is hiding a guilty secret or is just nervous. Police work should be based on facts and evidence but if a policeman ignores his gut instinct a lot more crime would go unsolved and suspects would walk free.

The Collins English Dictionary defines gut instinct as "*an instinctive feeling, as opposed to an opinion or idea based on facts.*"

"*For all the wonders of modern technology, there is no substitute for the gut instinct of a skilled police officer*".

In the 1970's without the sophisticated forensic technology available today, gut instinct was often the trigger that made policemen look harder for evidence and facts rather than accepting things on face value.

During the handover there would be a need to have a car available in central Durban to respond to any urgent matter, hence the early car. Each shift would have one member start an hour earlier than the rest of the shift to be available during the changeover period. Sergeant Vince Zimmerman was the early car of D shift in

April 1973 but as his dog was injured, I joined him as the driver with patrol dog Bruno.

Around 8.30 pm we received a call to go to a fire in the Stamford Hill area. I drove down Sydenham Road and turned left into Musgrave Road at which time Zimmerman saw a man jump into a Valiant car and drive up Sydenham Road in the direction we had just come from. He immediately said, "Turn around. Follow that car", and I did a quick U-turn.

In a glance, there was just something about the man, his appearance and demeanour that said, "Check this man and the car out". Chrysler Valliant's were a popular and powerful six-cylinder car capable of quick acceleration and top speeds. There were a number in use in the Flying Squad. I raced up behind the Valiant and tried to draw alongside with Zimmerman signalling the driver to pull over. His response was to speed up and take off turning into Essenwood Road proceeding at high speed in a southerly direction. I accelerated after him as Zimmerman contacted Radio Control to check the registration number for outstanding cases, or if it was a stolen car. Radio Control called other vehicles with a view to blocking the Valiant near the wide Berea Road flyover but as it was shift change, few vehicles were available.

As the two vehicles approached the intersection with St. Thomas Road we noticed that the traffic lights were on red and cars had stopped ahead of us. This may have been an opportunity to block the vehicle and stop the driver. The suspect driver saw the potential blockage and moved onto the other side of the road travelling directly at oncoming traffic at high speed and went through the intersection without touching brakes or considering the very real likelihood of crashing into another vehicle with the probability of killing or injuring other people.

Forty years after this incident police services across the world would have protocols which would result in a chase of this nature being called off for public safety reasons; but this was 1973 and common sense was supposed to apply. We were both conscious of the threat that the Valiant posed to the public, but it made us more determined to end the chase as quickly as possible. We only had our gut instinct to rely on as there was nothing more than reckless driving as a potential charge at that time. There had to be something more to it. The chase approached the Berea Road intersection. The lights were on red and traffic was backing up, but this time oncoming traffic was blocking the Valliant's route in the opposite lanes. The Valiant driver decided to mount a central island and scrape past the stationary vehicles in front of him and he sped across the intersection. I followed, after a brief hesitation to look out for other cars entering the intersection.

Zimmerman then stuck the upper part of his body out the window, drew his revolver, steadied himself and fired a shot which went through the rear window of the Valiant starring the glass. The Valiant jinked to the left as the driver instinctively ducked. Zimmerman fired a second shot as the two vehicles travelled at almost 100 kilometres per hour. The second shot went into the rear window and all the glass fell out giving a view of the driver who was ducking as he heard the shot, taking his foot off the accelerator and slowing down. The Valiant driver looked up and saw that he was approaching Clark Road, so he turned left to avoid travelling in a straight line providing an easier target.

The squad car pulled closer to the Valiant as I attempted to get on its right side to afford Zimmerman the chance of a clear shot at the driver, or to point the gun at him to get him to stop and surrender. This had no effect on the driver who accelerated so Zimmerman fired further shots at him shattering the back window behind the driver, and the driver's window. The suspect driver instinctively ducked as shots were fired but as he looked up, he suddenly saw that the road ahead was closed off with road works and barriers. It was too late to take further evasive action and the Valiant rocketed through the barriers, dropping down onto a new road that was under construction, hitting a raised manhole cover and blowing out two of his tyres. He still attempted to race away with pieces of tyre flying up as his rims bit into the gravel road base.

I drew alongside the Valiant and rammed it. The driver opened his door whilst it was still moving and tried to jump out. Zimmerman was hanging out the window of the squad car and tried to grab the man, but he pulled free and ran off. I released Bruno who was highly excited by the chase and sound of shots. He took off after the suspect at high speed, launching himself into the air and grabbing his arm in his jaws as the two crashed to the ground. Bruno hung onto the man until I grabbed him and arrested him, put the handcuffs on and then locked the suspect in a spare kennel of the squad car whilst we worked out what was going on.

Radio Control confirmed that the registration was not on the stolen list, so someone had to go to the Licensing Office to check the card index to see if the number plates were false. Shooting incidents had to be reported and the scene visited by an officer who would conduct an investigation to see if the use of a firearm was justified and lawful, as well as briefing a senior officer on standby.

Brigadier Mildenhall examines the shot up stolen Valiant: April 1973

A senior detective officer on standby would also have to be informed. At that stage we had a problem in that whilst we followed our instinct and the suspects' response was highly unnatural, there was only a potential driving violation that may not have justified the use of a weapon.

Other police vehicles began to arrive at the scene. One of them was the legendary Detective Sergeant Davidtz of the Murder and Robbery squad who was on the air and heard the car chase. Davidtz was a twenty five year veteran and a Zulu linguist who had an informer network that took years to build up. The Murder and Robbery squad investigated serious robberies usually involving firearms carried out by gangs with previous criminal records and who did not care who got in their way. Davidtz took one look at the suspect and said, "Hello Augustine. We have been looking for you".

We both felt relieved. The worry about overstepping the mark was replaced with the after-effects of the adrenaline rush. The Divisional Inspector, Brigadier Mildenhall who lived in the area came out to the scene and conferred with Davidtz as further information came to hand. Newspaper reporters and photographers arrived on the scene after receiving a tip off and photographed the scene with articles appearing in the Natal Mercury newspaper the following morning.

Sergeant Vince Zimmerman looks through the shattered rear window of the stolen Valiant

Radio Control reported that the vehicle registration was false as the records were not assigned to a Valiant. A short while later after looking at a list of stolen Valiants, it was confirmed that the car had been stolen 3 days earlier and fitted with false plates. It was confirmed by Davidtz that Augustine was part of a gang of hard core criminals who had carried out an armed robbery of a six thousand rand payroll the previous week in Wentworth, a suburb to the South of Durban. During the robbery Augustine's gang had fired 3 shots at an employee narrowly missing him. He was also wanted in connection with a massive Post Office theft in Umtata. It was suspected that the Valiant had been stolen to be used as a getaway car in another planned robbery.

All in all, this was a good case with a good outcome. A dangerous criminal was apprehended, and no member of the public was hurt despite the high risk. Police gut feeling had been proven correct. We felt vindicated that Augustine would not be at large to shoot anyone who stood in his way during a robbery but we were also left with an understanding of what the consequences would have been if we had got it wrong, if an innocent person was hurt during the chase or if the suspect was not a serious wanted criminal.

13

HIT AND RUN KILLER

In 1969 Sergeant Vince Zimmerman was stationed at Montclair Police Station, primarily a residential suburb to the South of Durban with an industrial area along South Coast Road. It was a weekend nightshift and Zimmerman was with a group of Police Reservists providing some hands on training involving vehicle stops and checks. Around midnight he saw a vehicle approaching with only one headlight, so he stepped into the road to stop the vehicle.

He was applying the concept of stopping people for minor transgressions of the law to educate where possible but also with the idea that petty offenders often commit more serious crimes, as their behaviour may indicate a disregard for any law and order. This concept became policy in New York during the tenure of Mayor Giuliani in the 1990's known as the Broken Windows Theory.

The vehicle was an open beach buggy driven by a young white male with a white male passenger. The front left headlamp and fender appeared to have been smashed in an accident and the driver was asked to explain what happened. Zimmerman recognised the driver as Brian Twiggs, a Montclair resident that he had met previously. Twiggs who smelt of alcohol said that he had struck a bollard on the side of the road. He said he was going home and would repair the damage before he used the vehicle again. Zimmerman noticed that the passenger was slumped and lying to the side in the front passenger seat with his head almost hanging out the vehicle. Twiggs said that the passenger had too much to drink and he was taking him home.

Zimmerman turned his attention to the passenger and in the street lights saw a wound on his forehead and blood coming from his ear. On closer inspection he appeared not to be drunk but seriously injured so Zimmerman called for an ambulance which arrived to assess the passenger identified as Anthony Smith, a resident of Glenwood, a neighbouring suburb. The ambulance crew ascertained that Smith required urgent medical attention and took him to the Addington Hospital on the Durban beachfront. Zimmerman then posed a series of questions to Twiggs to find out what happened. He asked where the accident happened, and Twiggs said that it was down on the Point near the beachfront. Zimmerman felt that Twiggs was being evasive so he contacted Radio Control to ask if they had any information of an accident on the beachfront or in town.

The report came back that a beach buggy had collided with a pedestrian on the Marine Parade in the vicinity of the Addington Hospital and the force of the collision had propelled a young woman into the windscreen of the beach buggy before dumping her onto the road killing her instantly. The beach buggy did not stop and fled the scene of the accident. A later examination of the accident showed that the passenger, Smith received his injuries as a result of the windscreen frame being driven back on impact with the pedestrian which hit Smith on the front of his head, causing massive internal bleeding. Twiggs had driven away to avoid being found to be driving under the influence of alcohol and all the consequences of his actions. He also failed to take make any attempt to get Smith any medical attention even though it was obvious that he was hurt and Twiggs was close the hospital that could have helped him.

Zimmerman warned Twiggs that he was arresting him on suspicion of drunken driving and culpable homicide resulting from the accident. He warned him of his rights in terms of judges' rules and took him to the Point Police Station. On the way, Twiggs said that he had a witness who could prove that he was innocent of the allegations as Smith was the driver and not him. Zimmerman detained Twiggs at Point and went to collect the witness to be taken separately to the Police Station to prevent any opportunity for colluding on an alibi. When Zimmerman got to the witness' flat he outlined that Twiggs had been in an accident and the witness could clarify events. The witness was not prepared to co-operate or discuss the matter with Zimmerman or reveal if he knew anything about the accident. Zimmerman then noticed a nude poster on the wall and a collection of magazines that were unlawful in South Africa's strict moral driven legal system.

Zimmerman told the "witness" that he was going to take him to Point Police Station to charge him for possession of illegal publications. On arrival at the station, Twiggs said to his witness in the presence of Zimmerman and others, "I killed a bird and pulled out to cool it!" The slang "pulled out" means he left the scene for things to cool off. Immediately after the accident, Twiggs had driven down a side street behind the Addington Hospital and parked his beach buggy leaving Smith unconscious in the front passenger seat to join the crowd at the accident scene so he could see what happened. He then decided to drive back to Montclair. The witness realised that he may get himself caught up in series of lies and did not provide any material support to assist Twiggs with an alibi. Twiggs claimed that Smith was the driver of the beach buggy when the accident occurred and that he only took over the driving to get Smith home.

Twiggs intended to take his seriously injured friend Smith to his home in Montclair rather than take him to Smith's home in Glenwood or a hospital. It got a whole lot worse for Twiggs when the hospital reported that Smith had died as a result of his injuries. Medical evidence presented in court proved that if Twiggs had taken Smith to hospital and he had received timely medical attention, Smith may have survived.

The case went to court some months later where Twiggs main defence was that Smith was the driver. This was patently untrue as the point of impact where the pedestrian was hit was on the front left of the vehicle which damaged the left headlamp and the left side of the windscreen which would have hit the passenger, not the driver. Zimmerman gave evidence of the events and particularly related the comments by Twiggs to his so-called witness in the charge office that he had killed a woman. The defence lawyer immediately protested to the judge that Zimmerman's evidence should be inadmissible as Twiggs was not properly informed of his rights and the admission to the policeman should be dismissed. Zimmerman and the prosecutor countered by arguing that the admission was made to his witness in the presence of the policemen after being properly cautioned.

Twiggs was found guilty of two counts of culpable homicide by causing death by dangerous driving. His defence was found to be improbable and untruthful and he was lacking in remorse which resulted in him being sentenced to four months imprisonment on each count. At the time and even on reflection forty years later, the sentence seems trivial in relation to the offence. The authorities and public attitude to road safety has come a long way since those days, and it should be noted that it was only a legal requirement for car manufacturers to fit seat belts in new vehicles in South Africa from the early 1970's, and mandatory for the public to wear them where they were fitted.

Anthony Smith's father and brother subsequently joined the Police Reservists and specialised in accident investigation and moving vehicle violations.

Twiggs' alcohol-affected mind may have accounted for his making some stupid, rash decisions both during the accident and immediately afterwards, but even with alcohol he should have realised at some time that he was making things worse, and that resulted in the death of his friend, Smith. Even more heinous was to try to blame his dead friend, and persist with an argument that showed no concern for others or remorse for his own actions. People with bad attitudes and who lack empathy for others seldom change or learn from their mistakes. Some years later Anthony Smith's father, whilst on duty as a Police Reservist, arrested Twiggs for riding a scooter without a licence.

14

DOGS ON THE RECEIVING END

Some members of the public may have thought that policemen and their dogs were a hard tool against criminals and softer methods may have worked better to effect an arrest or solve a crime. Solving a crime after a criminal has left the scene is time consuming and manpower intense. Detectives had limited science and forensic tools to support their efforts and criminals often got away to commit serious crime again, often causing injury or emotional trauma to victims.

The most efficient method of solving crime and preventing future crime was to arrest the suspects at the time of an offence or shortly afterwards when evidence and exhibits could be gathered to support a successful prosecution. This was the role of the Dog Unit, the first responders to crime in progress. The newspaper reports gave factual accounts of arrests and some members of the public may have thought that the police went in with odds stacked in their favour. This perception however did not take into account that many of the criminals had carefully chosen their intended victims, targeted the items they wished to steal and knew the area with various escape routes. Using police dogs also meant that suspects may give up rather than run for it, and police may then have less reason to resort to using firearms.

Police responding to crimes in progress did not always know the area well, how many criminals were operating, or if they were armed. The Dog Unit knew that time was crucial when a report of a crime in progress was reported. They had to get to the scene, anticipate how to approach the scene and respond to what they found, usually just the dog and Handler and Crew whilst waiting for back up that may be some minutes away.

Things did not always go the way of the policemen or their dogs. Dogs were injured and some criminals did not care if they hurt or killed a dog or Handler to get away.

In the early hours of 17 July 1973 Radio Control received a phone call from a resident near the Parkhill Shopping Centre in Old North Coast Road that they heard noises coming from the centre and they suspected that shops were being broken into. Sergeant Dan Malan and his dog Rinty were despatched to attend. I was not too far off and informed Control that I would attend as back up. Malan informed Control that he was about a minute away and I was probably about a minute behind him. I informed Control and Malan knew that I would be right behind him.

As Malan's squad car approached the Centre he saw three males run out of the shops crossing the road towards an area of overgrown vacant land. Malan stopped the car, released Rinty and gave chase. The men had over a hundred metres start and disappeared into the gloom heading up a slight rise to a railway line. There was diffused light near the railway line and Malan saw them running along the tracks with Rinty closing in. Rinty tackled one of the men and held onto his sleeve. Malan saw that the man had a panga (machete) and he was chopping at the dog. He hit the dog once and raised the panga to strike again, at which stage Malan drew his service revolver and shot the man in his left shoulder. The man fell and was disarmed. The other two suspects ran into the bush as they were exposed on the railway line.

When I arrived at the Centre, I saw Malan's squad car with the doors open and I realised that he was in pursuit of suspects. I took

Bruno out the kennel and released him. The scent of Malan, his dog and the suspects would have been incredibly fresh and strong for Bruno. He ran across the road without hesitation and through a rough patch on the vacant land, dropping his nose to the ground from time to time. I was running behind him and saw Malan on the railway line. He had handcuffed the suspect and briefly told me what happened. He wanted to take Rinty to the vet but there was still the whereabouts of the other suspects.

I released Bruno in the direction that Malan indicated the other suspects had run. Bruno went into the bush and after a few seconds began to bark. He had found another suspect about 30 metres away from the spot where the shot suspect was held. We decided to get the suspects back to the Centre and lock them in the cars so Rinty could get to the vet. The third suspect seemed to have run off and made good his escape rather than going to ground to hide. The Greenwood Park Station van arrived and arranged to take the injured man to hospital. The wound was relatively minor which may have been due to old ammunition or that the .38 revolver was underpowered compared to 9mm pistols.

I then proceeded to check shops in the Centre and found that three of the shops had been broken into. It appeared that items from the shops had been removed. There was nothing hidden outside the shops so our guess was that the suspects would have taken items across the road and hidden them in the overgrown vacant land and then gone back into the shops to take more goods. Other police members from Greenwood Park arrived on the scene and we found bundles of goods removed from the stores concealed in the undergrowth.

The exhibits and the second suspect were taken to the Police Station and detained. We were all pleased to hear that the vet had found that Rinty had relatively minor injuries that were stitched and treated. The panga man seemed to have not been able to get a clear hit on Rinty with the blade side of his weapon. It could have been a very different outcome. A full-blooded strike with the blade of the panga would probably kill or seriously injure a dog or a man. I had previously seen victims hit with a panga at crime scenes, and I had been to hospital casualty where I'd seen gaping wounds often accompanied by broken bones due to an attack with a panga.

Incidents of this nature brought it home that not every case could have a happy ending and that our uniform was not a superman suit. We had to be both alert and carefully confident in our ability and experience to assess the risks we faced with each complaint.

———

I had much empathy when a colleague's dog was injured but it was something else when my own dog was injured. There are a range of emotions ranging from anger, a need for retribution, and fear of losing a companion that would literally die for you.

On a Sunday afternoon in April 1975, whilst listening on the radio, I heard that the Durban North detectives wanted a Dog Handler to assist them near the Kwa Mashu Township as back up in their search for a suspected car thief who had run into the bush as they approached his house. Sergeant Flip Holtzhausen and Kuno were covering the North Durban area so he was despatched to meet the detectives. In such circumstances, the detectives would usually have information that a suspect was in a house and there may be friends of the suspect to interfere in the search and arrest. Car thieves often had a few stolen cars on hand, and we could expect them to be runners. It made sense to be accompanied by a dog for such an eventuality. The presence of a dog would also make friends and neighbours less likely to want to interfere.

In this case the detectives had approached the suspect's house without a dog and Handler and the suspect had fled into some nearby bush. Holtzhausen was taken to an area where detectives had taken up positions around a large perimeter hoping to contain the suspect. Kuno was sent into the bush area to look for the suspect. There was a thicket of thorny Lantana weed that got Kuno's attention as he burrowed under the thorns. Holtzhausen

and the detectives heard barking and shouting and shortly thereafter Kuno came out of the bush bleeding from a stab wound.

I heard Holtzhausen report over the radio that Kuno had been
stabbed and asked Control to get Amos & Clow Vets to standby for
his injured dog as he was on his way to the surgery. The detectives
asked for another dog handler to come to the scene to help with
flushing the suspect out. As the shift leader, I decided to deal with
this myself.

I was shown where Kuno had exited the bush and Bruno and I
looked to see if there was another way in. The bush was thick and
thorny, and the suspect must have torn himself to pieces to get
right in there. I called on him to come out threatening to send
Bruno in. I was reluctant to do so after Kuno had been injured but
mechanised equipment would have been needed to chop a way in.
Even using handheld slashers would not have made much
headway and it was not an option for any of the policemen to try
to climb in. Bruno was pretty smart, and I thought that if I sent
him in he would bark at the man and keep his distance to avoid
being hurt and get the man to crawl out.

I heard Bruno bark and it sounded as though the man was
about 10 meters ahead of me but I could not see anything in the
thick thorny weed. The barking and shouting went on for a few
minutes and then Bruno appeared from another side of the bush.
He was limping and I saw blood running down his head. I touched
his back and it felt wet and sticky. I knew that he had been stabbed
twice. I was angry with the suspect and myself as I had sent my pal
into a dangerous situation without providing close back up.

I had to get him to the vet quickly. I did not know if the stab
wound on his back had penetrated any vital organs. I told the
detectives that I was leaving, and they had to find another way of
getting the suspect out. I got to the vets' surgery just after they
finished with Kuno who was going to recover. I stayed with Bruno
as they shaved fur off the affected areas and examined the wounds.
No vital organs had been penetrated and after cleaning the
wounds, he was stitched. Both dogs would remain at the vet for a
few days before we took them back to the kennels at Cato Manor

and they returned to duty after a period of sick leave of around ten days.

Bruno's stab wounds to head and back treated by the Vet: April 1975

As I left the vet, I was informed that the detectives had managed to arrest the suspect and in addition to the car theft charges he would face two cases of malicious damage to property as the dogs were defined as state property. The detectives had gone after the suspect before asking for the dog and when he had run off, we were asked to tidy up an arrest that went wrong. I have no idea how they got the suspect. I surmise that he would have been bitten by both dogs and torn to pieces by the thorns and may have decided to come out. The way I felt at the time, threatening to burn him out may not have been a bad idea and that would probably have worked.

15

UNUSUAL CRIME SCENE

One would think that some places would never be a target for criminals, but I have come to the conclusion that you can never rule anything out. Even the most obscure places may have something that is attractive or valuable to a criminal.

The Fitzsimons Snake Park was situated at the northern end of the Golden Mile near the Natal Command Military Headquarters and had been a major Durban landmark and tourist attraction since 1938. The building had the outside characteristics of a fort with 10 foot high walls, whilst the inside had a ticket office, display cages, a breeding section, and a very large pit surrounded by a wall that had trees and bushes where a variety of snakes lived in semi natural conditions. There was a similar smaller pit that housed several crocodiles.

Although the park focused on South African snakes, there were others from different parts of the world, like the Anaconda, as well as spiders, lizards, tortoises, turtles, and scorpions that could be viewed by the paying public. During the summer the park received several calls a day from "terrified Durbanites" who had spotted snakes in their gardens or homes. The Snake Park staff would provide education to schools as well as help the hospitals in identifying snakes when people had been bitten, enabling them to administer the correct antivenom.

The Snell Parade continued northwards from the Snake Park for about a kilometre to the Umgeni River Mouth. The area between the beach and the road had sand dunes with drought resistant succulent plants to stabilise the dunes and prevent sand moving onto the road. These were ecologically sensitive so the Council Parks and Beaches department surrounded the plant covered dunes with fencing to keep people out so the plants could flourish.

On a July afternoon in 1973 I was patrolling slowly along the Snell Parade opposite the Natal Command when a man emerged suddenly from the dune bushes and jumped over the fence landing right next to the squad car. My crew and I stopped him as it appeared that someone had chased him out of the bushes by the way he was looking over his shoulder as he cleared the fence. We noticed that that he had blue fluff in his hair that appeared to have come from a blanket.

This needed more investigation. The man said that he had been sleeping in the bush and he heard a noise that frightened him. We decided to take him with us onto the beach and see if we could find anything out of the ordinary. I took Bruno out the car but as the man was reluctant to show us where he was sleeping we walked along the fence until we found a small hole that had been made by cutting some of the chain link fence and then unravelling an area big enough for a man to crawl through.

I crawled through and Bruno followed me leaving the man with my crew. We only went about 10 paces into the bush when I saw a blue blanket that seemed to match the fluff fibres in the man's hair. To my surprise under the blanket I found a safe about 4 foot square that had signs that someone had been trying to pry it open with a hammer and chisel. The tools were next to the safe. My first suspicion was that the safe had been stolen from a nearby hotel and given the size and weight of the safe it must have required a few people to have carried it to the hiding spot in the bush.

Bruno was alert and it seemed to indicate to me that there may be other people hiding in the bush. At that moment my Crew called out that there were two men trying to climb over the fence. Bruno and I spotted them as we moved towards the fence. Bruno barked and the men decided to give up. The three men were taken to the squad car where I contacted Radio Control and reported my findings. The Point patrol van arrived to take the prisoners and the detectives were contacted and asked if they had any reports of a stolen safe.

To my great surprise the reply was that the safe had been stolen from the Snake Park over the weekend. The men would have climbed over the high outer wall, broken into the office and manhandled the safe out the building, along the beach and into the fenced bushy dunes over a distance of around 200 metres. I was even more amazed that Africans, who have a great fear of snakes, had taken the risk to have gone into the Snake Park where one wrong step could have had very serious consequences. The only conclusion that I could come to was that at least one of the suspects must have worked at the Snake Park at some time.

When the safe was opened it contained R360 in cash and other valuables. The cash amount was the equivalent of about two month's salary for me at the time.

In 1974 two of my friends from Police College completed the dog course and joined the Dog Unit. Doug Linden, who was a student with me at Umbilo, returned with Ceazer, whilst Mervin Van Rensburg returned with Nero.

Shortly after joining the Dog Unit, Van Rensburg received a report from Radio Control at around 11pm that a member of the public who lived in a tall block of flats overlooking the Snake Park had seen someone climb over the rear wall of the Snake Park and then saw torch lights in the building. Van Rensburg drove to the area and walked around to the rear of the building. He was not keen on snakes, but he climbed up on to the top of the wall and sat there in the dark. He was not going to climb down into the open yard area as that would have been very foolhardy.

He was not in position very long when a young man climbed out of the courtyard and onto the wall near Van Rensburg. He called on the man to stop. On seeing the policeman, the suspect put a gloved hand into a sack he was carrying, withdrew a snake and made as if to throw it at the policeman. Van Rensburg quickly drew his service pistol and told him in no uncertain terms that he would shoot him if he tried to throw the snake at him. He directed the man to climb down and secure the bag so that nothing got out.

Van Rensburg reported back to Radio Control who contacted the person who reported the intrusion. The informant was friendly with the Snake Park proprietors and arranged for them to meet the police on the scene. The owner of the Snake Park said he had noticed that some of his rare snakes were disappearing, and suspected that someone was coming over the wall at night. The thief was a reptile enthusiast who had a collection of snakes at home and was selling them to his friends. His unusual hobby however did not stop him from being detained and prosecuted as a warning to others.

Some months after this event, another group of new Dog Handlers passed out from Police Dog School with their dogs.

Constables Pieter Du Plooy and Mervin Van Rensburg of the class of '74

As was the custom, the new arrivals were posted with older members to induct them for the first few shifts and so Constable Giepie van Rensburg was posted to crew alongside the experienced and newly promoted Sergeant Mervin Van Rensburg; no relation!

On shift they heard that a woman had reported a large snake in her house. Giepie told Mervin that he was very interested in snakes and knew how to handle them. He asked Mervin to take them to the complaint. On their arrival the complainant took Giepie to point out where she saw the snake, whilst Mervin waited outside. After some time, a triumphant Giepie came out holding a large snake tightly behind the head, and asked Mervin to take him and the snake to the Snake Park.

Mervin thought about the request and the implications of driving the car whilst his namesake sat next to him holding a large snake. What if the snake got loose or if he had to brake suddenly and Giepie lost control of the snake? Mervin decided that was not a good idea and called for a station van to take policeman and snake to the Snake Park in the back of the van where any unexpected accidents did not endanger anyone else.

It seems that snakes polarise people with those who like snakes being strongly positive, whilst those who fear snakes having equally strong but negative feelings. Our shift had two real snake lovers with Constable Basie Cronje who worked as a Controller with the Radio Control indoor staff, and Giepie Van Rensburg. Both had mildly venomous pet snakes at home. During the Durban summer, with daytime temperatures reaching 30 degrees Celsius snakes would become more active and hence visible, prompting not only calls to the Snake Park but also to Police Radio Control. One steamy summer afternoon Basie received a phone call from an Indian lady in Clare Estate, west of the city, who reported a big snake in her yard.

The two snake lovers decided to deal with this one themselves. They got permission from the Duty Officer for Basie to be picked up and attend the report with his fellow snake lover, Giepie. On their arrival, the anxious lady took them to the rear of her property and pointed out an area where an outhouse had been demolished. She related that she saw the snake near a pile of corrugated iron sheets and the two eager snake fans tip toed up to the sheeting. They started carefully and quietly moving the iron sheeting until they saw a tail sticking out from under a sheet.

They realised from the olive brown colouring that the snake was probably a black mamba, one of the deadliest snakes in the world. Black mambas typically grow from two to three meters in length with some growing up to four metres. Mambas are known to be skittish, often unpredictable, and to be able to move as fast as a running horse. The venom is predominantly neurotoxic, with symptoms often becoming apparent within 10 minutes, and collapse in humans within 45 minutes or less. Without appropriate anti-venom treatment, symptoms lead to respiratory failure, which leads to cardiovascular collapse and death. Both policemen knew this, yet they were determined to capture this snake.

Basie said he would take the snake by its tail and pull it out so that Giepie could grab it behind the head when it appeared from under the sheeting. Basie took hold of the snake's tail and pulled it out a few feet, then a further three feet but there was still no sign of the head. For most people that would have been one of those "Oh shit!" moments where they would have considered giving up, but not these two. With a further tug the snake's head appeared, enabling the policeman to grab it quickly and firmly behind the head. They felt quite pleased with themselves and decided to take the snake to Radio Control to show their colleagues before taking it to the Snake Park.

Both policemen had hold of the snake but when it came to having to drive the squad car back, only one would have to control the snake as they never had a strong bag to safely contain it. The snake wrapped its long body around Giepie's arms, making most of us wonder who was holding who. When they got to Radio Control, a photo was taken with Giepie holding his arm up at full extension holding the snake's head whilst its tail dangled down reaching the ground, with a loop of an extra foot. It was a ten-foot monster.

Following these events it was decided that any further reports of snake sightings would be referred directly to the Snake Park since they were properly equipped to catch snakes and there was less risk of something going wrong.

16

FORD RANCHERO CHASE

I n the summer of 1974, I was patrolling near our old family house in Manning Road at about 3am, and noticed a Ford Ranchero with a boat and trailer in tow. The Ford Ranchero was essentially a van which was shaped like a sedan motor car with a bench front seat for the driver and two passengers, with a low profile rear for luggage which usually had a plastic canopy fitted to preserve its sleek lines. It had a powerful six cylinder engine that had terrific acceleration and a good top speed.

The Ranchero appeared to have just pulled off from the side of the road. I flicked my lights at it since it had no lights, however it took off at high speed. I immediately gave chase and after about 300 yards when speed had built up it had to turn a corner, but the trailer and boat came adrift, mounted the pavement and launched itself into a hedge and came to rest. The Ranchero sped off again, so I carefully manoeuvred around the trailer and continued the pursuit. I switched off my lights so the driver would not know how close I was. We raced through the deserted streets for about twenty seconds when I realised that I had lost him. I had been unable to get the registration number but I had broadcast the details of the Ranchero to Radio Control. Other cars searched the area, nevertheless the vehicle had disappeared.

I went back to the boat and trailer, realising that it must have been stolen as no rational person would have acted that way. I arranged for a colleague to check the vehicle registration for the owner's details. It was later reported that the owner was Neville Slot who lived about 6 houses away from our old home in Manning Road and at the place where I first saw the vehicle and trailer. I knew Neville from the time that we lived in the area and he confirmed that it was his property. The trailer had been removed from his garage after the lock to the garage had been forced. I arranged for Neville to open a case at the Umbilo Police Station.

The following night whilst on patrol close to midnight I spotted a Ford Ranchero about 4 blocks away from Manning Road. I raced up to the vehicle and indicated for the driver to pull over. He tried to race off, but I quickly cut in front of him and forced him to stop. I called for back-up as I was alone in the vehicle and colleagues arrived in a few minutes. The occupants looked to be in their early 20s, and comprised of 2 or 3 young drifter type white males and a female. I searched the vehicle and found a couple of jerry cans in the rear with a length of rubber hose that was still wet with petrol. I suspected that they had been stealing petrol from vehicles in the area. I questioned them about this and a radio tape player that I found in the back of the vehicle.

They were very evasive and could not give me a straight answer for their possession of these items, and neither could they give me satisfactory information about where they lived or worked so I decided to arrest them for possession of stolen property. I took them and detained them at Umbilo and left a statement for the detectives. I went off duty at 7am and went to bed. I received a phone call from the detectives some hours later who advised me that they had brought Neville Slot down to the station to search though the Ranchero. Neville had found a number of screwdrivers which he was able to identify from marks that he had previously made on them. The tools had been inside his boat and had not been recovered when the boat was returned to him. We now had the link to the theft of the boat and trailer, and for good measure, the Ranchero had false licence plates and had been stolen.

Wearing summer uniform with Bruno at Valiant squad car M24:
December 1974

One of the outcomes of the 1973 Yom Kippur War and ongoing unrest in the Middle East was that petrol had a steep hike in price and supplies became less reliable. The era of cheap petrol was gone and as petrol supplies remained uncertain, petrol restrictions were put in place in 1974 which lasted for over a year. Measures included the closing of petrol stations at night and lower speed limits to use fuel more sparingly. This in turn led to increases in theft by siphoning petrol from parked cars using hoses and jerry cans. The motor industry responded by fitting new cars with metal nets just inside the petrol cap to prevent hoses being inserted.

17

THE FOLLY OF REPEATING THE CRIME

Sunday nights were usually quiet from a complaint point of view, but there would be the usual housebreakings and car thefts in the early hours of the morning. Around midnight on one Sunday night in 1974, I received a report of an intruder alarm at Greenacres in central Durban. Greenacres was a large upmarket four storey department store that had shop frontages in Smith Street and West Street, with Greenacres Passage down the one side. The Greenacre family was very prominent with three members of the family elected as Mayor of Durban; the first in the 1870's. The department store was built at the start of the 1900's and was a typical department store of the time with wooden framed glass display cabinets with a wide range of goods.

I drove to the Smith Street entrance and noticed that the glass front door had been smashed by a brick which was lying inside the shop near the door. I released Bruno into the shop, and he responded immediately by running down to the West Street side of the shop as he followed scent. At the far end of the shop was a jewellery counter which had watches, bracelets and chains on display. The display counters had been smashed and I could see that a lot of items had been removed.

I searched the ground floor and then heard the alarm company keyholder arrive. We checked the alarm panel which indicted that alarms on the ground floor only had been activated. We concluded that the suspects had not bothered with other items and had been solely focussed on the jewellery as high value and easily transportable and saleable items. The criminals had concentrated on speed by getting in and out quickly before anyone could respond to the alarm. The shop manager arranged for a security guard to be posted at the broken door until it could be repaired the following day.

I was working night shift again the following Sunday and received another report of an alarm at Greenacres around midnight. I drove straight to the Smith Street entrance and saw the smashed glass of the front door with the brick lying a few feet inside the shop. I thought to myself, "same modus operandi, same time, same place and therefore same suspects", as I released Bruno into the store. It was a replay of the previous Sunday with the jewellery counter ransacked and cleaned out. The criminals had already left and when the keyholder from the alarm company arrived, we examined the alarm control panel and the area on the ground floor was the only affected area. The quick entry, focus on high end goods and getting out quickly had worked for them once again.

I was on duty again the following Sunday night and I wondered if the suspects would push their luck with another smash and grab at the same door around the same time. Two break-ins on consecutive Sunday nights at the same time and same place seemed too much of a coincidence. I mulled it over for a while and eventually had a feeling that these blokes were prob-ably so pleased with their success that they would try it again. I asked the Radio Control Indoor Supervisor to phone the alarm company and to ask them to watch out for the Greenacres alarm. I requested that they not waste time to write out complaint forms but to just come on the air and announce "Alarm at Greenacres."

I patrolled very close to Greenacres and received the call within a few minutes of midnight. I was at the Smith Street door in less than a minute and saw the broken glass with the trademark brick lying inside the door. I released Bruno into the shop, and he ran along a scent trail straight to the jewellery counter as I ran after him. I saw Bruno disappear behind the counter as I approached the area. I suddenly saw a man jump up screaming from behind the counter. He had a bag in his hand which contained watches and chains, and Bruno had latched on to his bum. I grabbed the man, searched him quickly for weapons and cuffed him. I then sent Bruno out to search the surrounding area as I expected the suspect to have at least one other accomplice.

At that moment, fellow Dog Handler Eivind Gjosund came in to give me back up, so I handed the suspect on to him. Bruno had picked up another scent at a nearby clothing section. He went behind a counter and I heard him bark, then a shout and a thud. The second suspect had backed in under the counter and was sitting with his legs crossed. Bruno had stuck his head under the counter and bitten him. He had shouted and jumped up bumping his head on the underside of the wooden counter. He then ran past the dog towards me holding the torn and bloody front of his trousers. He was holding his penis in his hand and it looked like Bruno had torn it rather badly.

I rushed the injured suspect off to hospital. When the nursing staff cleaned the area, it became apparent that he was not too badly damaged. The doctor and nurses applied a few stitches and said that he was fine to go to the Police Station. The Zulu nurses were not sympathetic with their tribal brother and could barely disguise their mirth. I was surprised by their reaction, but many of them were molested and robbed by "tsotsis" (young gangsters) at the bus ranks from time to time so they did not have much sympathy for him. They told him to take a course of antibiotics that they gave him and advised him not to use his willy for several weeks.

The two criminals had been smart in planning and executing the break ins, which were targeted at high value, light weight, easily converted to cash items, and had done so in minutes before they left the crime scene. Their folly was to repeat the successful formula on consecutive Sunday nights, at the same time and at the same point of entry. What probably also contributed to their capture was that the same police shift was on duty on the consecutive Sunday nights as their raids on the store. If different shifts had been on duty, the knowledge of the modus operandi may not have been recognised or anticipated that another break in was probable. The two men had previous convictions for Housebreaking and were sentenced to five years imprisonment.

———

Some months after arresting the Greenacres suspects, I received a report from Radio Control around 2am that a resident in a block of flats had heard noises at a café at the corner of Bartle Road and Fenniscowles Road, Umbilo. I headed in that direction knowing that I would have to make an external check of the premises. Control would have told the person who phoned in the report to remain indoors and remain on the line, not to put any lights on or to make any noise as a dog car was coming to investigate. I stopped a distance away and approached the shop on foot with Bruno. The shop was on the ground floor of a three-story block of flats with the main entrance right on the corner of the intersection. I approached the front door and it seemed to be locked and intact. I shone my torch and looked into the store with particular attention to the till area and the cigarette racks behind the till, and then at the fanlight windows, but they all seemed intact. The property comprised a Portuguese market garden and a general dealer store. I looked for a rear entrance to the shop which I found on the side near the entrance to the foyer of the flats.

The door was locked but there were visible signs that someone had tried to force the lock as there were marks in the woodwork made by a screwdriver or crowbar. I suspected that the criminal had seen me approach as Bartle Road was long and straight with a good view down the road notwithstanding my slow approach with the car lights off and stopping some distance away. I noted that there was no alarm system installed in the shop. I reported my finding to Radio Control who would have passed my report on to the person who phoned in the complaint.

Conventional wisdom would expect that the criminal had made his escape and would call off his break in and go home or try another target, especially as residents of the flats above the shop may have heard him. Something told me to continue to patrol in the general area in case I could spot someone hiding in the area or find someone in possession of housebreaking implements. Possession of housebreaking implements in suspicious circumstances and being unable to give a satisfactory account for that possession was an offence. If we found someone with a crowbar, screwdriver, gloves or similar items in the middle of the night without a reasonable excuse, we would detain them on that charge to give the local police station detectives an opportunity to check the suspects' fingerprints against any reported crimes. There was a reasonable rate of success when looking to match suspects with housebreaking implements and outstanding cases.

Some two hours later, the resident in the flats who had phoned in the original report called again and reported more noise near the shop door. This time I approached from the bottom end of Fenniscowles Road as that was around the corner from the door that had been damaged. I walked to the door and found that it had been forced open. I pushed it open wider and called out before releasing Bruno into the store and following him in. The shop had the usual corner store items for sale as well as a large vegetable and fruit section with various items stacked in boxes with large piles of watermelon and pumpkin. Bruno indicated to me by his behaviour that scent was fresh, but was the suspect still in there hiding or had he left?

The various smells of vegetables and herbs could mask the scent of a suspect, however I saw Bruno using his paw to dig at the pumpkin pile, so I started to lift pumpkins off the top. Bruno started to growl and as I lifted another pumpkin, I caught a glimpse of clothing. I reached over to pull on the clothing when suddenly the pumpkin pile broke open as the suspect kicked out, sending pumpkin rolling and falling all over. The suspect had heard me approaching and had burrowed under the pumpkin pile to hide. Bruno tried to jump in as the man, whilst still lying on the ground, kicked out sending Bruno flying. I stepped over a mass of spinning and rolling pumpkins to grab the man when he kicked me in the groin. I thought, "Shit, that hurt!" The suspect was still kicking out at Bruno and me, so I drew my wooden baton from my pocket and was going to whack him on the leg to overpower him and arrest him. As I swung at him, I slipped as a pumpkin smacked against my leg and I ended up hitting myself on my shin. That was almost as sore as being kicked in the bollocks, but by that time Bruno jumped in and grabbed the man by his trouser leg and started tugging on him. The man was now distracted by the dog, so I grabbed him and dragged him to his feet, got Bruno to sit behind me and handcuffed the man.

I then took stock of items in the shop. On searching the man, I found cash in notes and a lot of coins in his pockets. The till had been emptied but he did not have much time to pack other valuables for removal. I was now faced with the problem of securing the premises until the owner could be found. Some shops had after hour's emergency telephone numbers displayed near the door that we could contact to get the owner to take charge of his premises. In some cases we had no means of contacting an owner. We did not have enough policemen to post at the store until the owner arrived so we would arrange for a Security Company to post a guard at the shop for which the owner or his insurance would be liable.

The suspect had been caught because he pushed his luck. He had a narrow escape the first time, but it was foolish enough to go back and try again. Some criminals were clever, some were cunning, some were dangerous and others, just plain stupid. The shop owner had his potential loss saved by an alert resident in the flats above, the suspect was in the cells, and I had a throbbing shin and tender groin. I suppose that was all in a night's work.

RESERVOIR HILLS GUNMAN

One of my colleagues, Sergeant Vince Zimmerman, or Zimmy as we called him, was severely injured in September 1975 when he was run down by a drunken driver. His leg was badly broken in several places and was repaired with a metal plate. The injury meant that his damaged leg would be shorter than the other leaving him with a permanent limp. Zimmy was not prepared to leave the Unit and take up a job at a Station.

He opted to have his leg surgically broken again and rotated to gain sufficient mobility to be able to remain a Dog Handler. The op nearly cost him his life due to medical complications, but after months of rehabilitation he returned to full duty in June 1976. He was a very smart policeman with a good knowledge of the law, and he had an easy rapport with the public. When he returned to duty after several months of convalescence, I placed him on my vehicle as my crew.

One weekday morning shift around lunchtime, we were patrolling in the Reservoir Hills area. We were due to go off duty in about an hour so we would patrol in the area for another 30 minutes before moving back to Cato Manor to book off the air and put our dogs in the kennels. Reservoir Hills was an affluent Indian residential area that suffered from daytime housebreaking as some of the houses had open veld in the immediate area and were remote from one another. Indian households usually had high value jewellery as it was the culture to have gold bracelets and chains as a dowry for even poor families. As a lot of the gold jewellery was worn by the wife, many housebreakings were carried out when people were at home. The victims would either be threatened with violence or assaulted and forced to reveal areas of hidden wealth.

I drove down towards the river along a road in an open area of veld that was still to be developed. I spotted a lone man walking along the road. He appeared to be coming from nowhere and going nowhere as there was nothing in the immediate area. I stopped next to him and immediately got out of the vehicle to talk to him. Some of my colleagues may have stayed in the car and asked questions of the man through the window, but my intuition was to get out where I had room to manoeuvre if I had to.

The man put his right hand in his pocket, and I grabbed it before he could remove it. I felt a pistol in his hand through the pocket material. He began to struggle violently to remove his hand and the pistol from his pocket. I shouted, "He has a gun" and reached backwards with my left hand and pulled open the kennel door to release Bruno who flew into the man. I could then concentrate my effort on getting the weapon safely from his pocket whilst the man was distracted with the dog chewing on his leg. I passed the pistol on to Zimmy who had exited the vehicle to run around to me. He was then able to search the man for any other weapons and to handcuff him. The weapon was a .25 silver pistol with a pearl coloured handle and had a round in the breech. I am convinced that if I had a relaxed attitude and had merely stopped next to him and spoke to him through the window of the squad car, he would have shot us both and taken our weapons. The pistol had been stolen from a house some weeks previously and had been used in the commission of several robberies.

The man was convicted of several counts of robbery and possession of an unlicensed firearm and sentenced to imprisonment for five to eight years for the prevention of crime. Having a proactive attitude is crucial in police work especially when you never know what you may run into.

Bruno with the Eric Gordon trophy for the most First Schedule arrests awarded for the 1973/4 year and shared with Pieter Du Plooy in 1974/5

19

THE VALUE OF GOOD NEIGHBOURS

As the Warrant Officer in charge of the shift, my main role was to manage and supervise my colleagues, to allocate them to various patrol areas and provided advice and guidance on issues of law or process. If there were insufficient crews to be assigned to the vehicles, I would ensure that my subordinates got them, so I often drove around accompanied only by Bruno and no crew. I still wanted to be in on the action and lead by example, so I would attend the more serious complaints or provide back up to my colleagues. If a crime in progress was reported, it would be up to the Dog Handler closest to the scene to get there first and back up would arrive thereafter. As I probably knew the greater Durban area better than anyone else, the closest vehicle was not always the first on the scene. I would take time to study maps and familiarise myself with short cuts and the quickest route at different times of the day or night.

In 1974, my parents had decided to downsize and sold the family home, moving into a block of flats. I decided to move into the single quarter barracks at Cato Manor where the Dog Unit headquarters and kennels were based. I would often get to work early ahead of a night shift, take Bruno out of his kennel, let him loose to do his business, and then place him in my car before I took the parade and assigned men to vehicles and patrol areas. I had completed my parade shortly after 9pm and booked on the air with Radio Control while my colleagues were getting their dogs out of the kennels. Control asked me to go to a house in Durban North, just off the Northway to investigate a possible housebreaking.

I was advised that neighbours knew that the parents were away on a holiday and the granny was looking after the two high school daughters. The neighbours also knew that the granny and girls had gone to a school event and that there should be nobody at home, when they observed lights switched on in various parts of the house. Thinking that the school event had been changed, they phoned the house to check if everything was OK. The phone was answered by an African male. They asked him who he was, and he replied that he was the domestic worker. They knew this to be incorrect and phoned Police Radio Control.

I drove to the address knowing that back up would be some minutes behind me. I stopped about 4 or 5 houses away and took Bruno out the kennel. I approached the front door on foot and saw that it was open and slightly ajar. Several suitcases were packed and standing just inside the door. I stepped in quietly with Bruno but knocked over one of the cases which hit the ground with a dull thud. A man stepped out from a bedroom up the passage and I saw that he had a camera and set of binoculars in a case draped over each shoulder. His eyes grew large as he saw me, and he ran off towards the back door. Most housebreakers would open the front and back doors of a house whilst they were removing items, so it gave them two escape options if they were surprised. I released Bruno to catch him and hold him as I wanted to catch him as close to the house as possible because I expected that he was not alone. If I ran off out the back door, a second suspect would use the time to escape through the front door.

I ran after the man expecting to find myself in the kitchen with an open rear door in front of me, but I heard a shout as he disappeared from sight, followed by a splash. I ran in the direction of the noise and saw that the man had been distracted by the dog chasing him and had run into the bathroom instead of the kitchen. Bruno had grabbed his leg as he ran into the room, and he had fallen into the bath which was half full of water with clothes that had been left to soak in washing powder. Bruno and the man were both in the bath thrashing up a lot of foam. I took the suspect out and handcuffed him. I ran back to the car and locked him in the spare kennel with one end of the cuffs locked to the metal kennel, and then ran back to the house to let Bruno search the house for additional suspects. The neighbours had been watching the events and had come to the house when they saw me run out with a prisoner.

As I got back to the house, the neighbour and his gardener, armed with sticks, were standing in the lounge. I could not release Bruno again as with the excitement of a tackle he may have gone for the neighbours, so I took him outside and tied his leash to the gate. I was speaking with the neighbours when the granny and two girls arrived. The crime scene was hard to manage as I had not yet completed my search and could not deal with things by myself with all the goings on. I was speaking to the granny and girls when I saw the one girl's eyes widen in horror as she looked over my shoulder. I followed her glance towards the full-length lounge curtains and saw the toecaps of a pair of shoes sticking out from underneath.

I held my fingers to my lips and spoke with a normal voice, requesting everyone to go outside. Back up had not yet arrived and I had no idea if the man behind the curtains was armed or not. I had to deal with this matter immediately and alone. I drew my pistol and crept silently up to the shape behind the curtains. I stuck the pistol barrel up against the form of the man's head and said, "Hands up!" The whole curtain trembled as the man shook from the surprise. I drew the curtain aside, turned the man around and pushed him to the ground so he was lying face down. I had already used my handcuffs on the first man and had no means of constraining him. At that moment a colleague rushed in with his dog as he had obviously been briefed by the family standing outside when he arrived.

We handcuffed the second suspect and placed him in a police vehicle. I could now manage the crime scene properly and proceeded to take all the necessary details for the case docket. I am sure that somewhere in the world there are two middle aged sisters who will remember the burglar behind the curtains in their lounge and relate the story to their children.

Good neighbours are an effective way to build safer communities. People who talk over the fence and keep an eye out for one another can make families less prone to crime and its consequences, but not all information from neighbours is helpful.

One early morning around 3am I received a report from control that asked me to go to a house in Manning road near to where I lived in the 1960s. The neighbour had phoned and reported that the family of the next door house was away on a week's holiday and was due to return in a couple of days. They heard a noise at the neighbour's house. They had looked out and seen lights go on and off.

I left my police vehicle 100 meters away from the house and approached on foot accompanied by Bruno and two colleagues. We entered the gate at the pavement and walked through the yard up to the front door. The house was in darkness and I listened at the door for any sound of activity within. One colleague went around the back of the house to keep an eye on a rear door and windows whilst another stood with me. I tried the front door handle and to my surprise it was not locked, and it opened. We felt a slight rush as it appeared that there were intruders in the house as the neighbour reported that they checked the house daily and everything was locked and secure the previous day.

We stepped quietly into the house with Bruno and stood for a while to listen for noise and to let our eyes become more accustomed to the dark. I then released Bruno who immediately went up the stairs of the double storey house towards the bedrooms. The layout of the house looked very similar to that of my old family home in Manning Road. I saw Bruno enter the main bedroom as I was quietly coming up the last few stairs. He immediately gave a subdued bark as I ran towards the room. He would have given a louder bark if he found someone doing something or hiding in the room, so I ran into the room not really knowing what I would find. I saw Bruno barking at a couple in bed who woke up with a start as I switched on the room light.

I saw at a glance that it must have been the authorised residents whose immediate fear at being woken by a barking dog changed to one of confused surprise to see a policeman in their bedroom at 3am. Their son and daughter came running into the main bedroom in a bit of a flap and were just as puzzled as their parents.

They took the incident in good humour once the shock wore off. They had found the holiday venue very poor and had decided to come home early without letting the neighbours who were watching their home know of the changed arrangements.

I do not think that the incident would have ruptured relations with the neighbours as the couple seemed very level-headed and saw the positive side of the intrusion. They also realised that they should have taken the basic precaution of locking the front door, as well as notifying their neighbours of their early return.

Over the next 10 to 20 years, the character of the area changed with rising incidents of crime and residents feared they could become victims. Most houses would build large walls at street level which would have made entry into the property very difficult. At that time however, the era of intercoms and CCTV cameras at street level and alarm systems inside the houses of middle class residents was still to come.

20

MURDER IN SUBURBIA

E arly on the evening of 29 May 1974, Radio Control Operator Janet Dorrington received a phone call from a male caller who told her, "I have just shot a bird." Dorrington thought that someone was playing the fool, so she asked him what type of bird he meant. The caller replied, "You know what I mean". Dorrington had worked as a call receiver at Radio Control for a number of years and was an experienced operator. Her overall impression was that the caller was very casual and not worried at all. Not being sure of what to make of this she took the address of the caller and went to the radio calling for any vehicle in the vicinity of Albert Park.

I heard a colleague say that he would attend so she outlined the nature of the conversation with the caller suggesting that she was not sure if the call was really a serious event or not. I decided that as I was not too far off that I would attend as back up to my colleague. I parked the squad car in Park Street near Kingston flats and walked up to flat 54. As I approached the flat door, I saw that it was open, and I noticed a bloody smear mark on the wall near the door. I was now extra alert and carefully looked into the flat. I could hear a voice in the lounge and as I walked in, I saw a white male aged about 40 talking on the phone. He had an open bottle of whisky in front of him and he was swigging directly from the bottle.

He saw me enter the front door and stopped his telephone conversation for a second and said, "In the bedroom", and pointed down the passage. I thought that my colleague had arrived and was in the bedroom, so I walked on to join him to see if the report was a hoax or not, leaving the man to continue his phone call. As I walked into the room, I saw a large woman lying on the bed with numerous bullet wounds and blood stains on her clothing. I checked for a pulse and quickly concluded that with the number of wounds on her torso that she was dead. I noticed a .32 revolver on the bed next to the body.

I realised that the cool and calm man in the lounge must have been the caller and he had shot a bird of the human variety. I wrapped the revolver in a handkerchief to preserve any finger-prints and put it into my large tunic pocket to keep it safe. I went into the lounge where the man was still talking on the phone and swigging whisky probably in the attempt to get his blood alcohol count raised as a defence of intoxication to claim that he did not know what he had done. I took the phone off him and put it down before turning to the man telling him what I had found and that I had reason to believe that he had unlawfully killed a person and that I was arresting him.

Police procedure requires that a person being arrested must be informed of his rights. In South Africa informing a person of his rights was called Judges' Rules and is very similar to warnings given on arrests by police in the UK and America. I informed him of his rights including the part that he does not have to say anything but that anything he said would be taken down and used in evidence. I asked him if he understood. He then said, "She is dead. I shot her six times. I emptied the gun against her... bang... bang...bang". He went further and said, "Although she is dead, she is still a fat fucking bitch". I took that down in my pocketbook and was surprised that whilst the words are very strong and shocking, his manner and speech was amazingly relaxed given the situation.

The man was identified as Patrick Grove-Mitchell and the dead woman as his live in partner, Yvonne Eva. At this time a colleague walked into the flat. I asked him to get back to Control and update them and request that the Murder and Robbery Unit attend as a firearm had been used. I took the bottle of whisky away from him to pass on to the detectives when they arrived. Detective Sergeant "Mielie" Pretorius arrived about 10 minutes later and was greeted by his nickname by Grove-Mitchell. Their paths had crossed some years earlier when Pretorius was investigating an abortion case.

The suspect then spoke to Pretorius saying that he had got into an argument at the drive-in which continued when he got home. He then shot Miss Eva six times adding that he was sorry. Other detectives arrived to support Pretorius and I then handed the crime scene and the revolver over to them and left. I wrote a full and detailed statement on my observations and the admissions made by the accused after warning him about his rights.

Some five months later I received a subpoena to appear in the Pietermaritzburg Supreme Court where Grove-Mitchell was being charged with murder. The South African law courts had a hierarchy based on the importance and severity of cases and the ability of each court to impose more severe sentences. I regularly gave evidence in Magistrates Courts for relatively minor cases whilst most of my cases were held in the Durban Regional Courts that could impose sentences of up to 15 years on habitual criminals who met certain criteria. Pietermaritzburg was the capital of the Province of Natal and the Provincial Supreme Court was based in the capital city. Each of the four provinces had a Supreme Court and there was a National Supreme Court known as the Appeal Court.

I attended court on the due date and on entering the witness box proceeded to read out my statement. When I got to the part about Grove-Mitchells comments, there was pandemonium in the court gallery and his defence attorney immediately jumped up and called upon the Judge to rule that my evidence was inadmissible on a point of law. The Judge then adjourned the court to consider the claim by the defence. I was told that I was excused, so I left and travelled back to Durban. Some weeks later I was informed by the police investigating officer that the Judge had ruled that my evidence was admissible as I had followed all the correct procedures and the accused had made voluntary admissions to me and to Pretorius.

The court judgement that Grove-Mitchell was found guilty of murder made the newspapers. The Judge, Mr Justice Hoexter who sat with two assessors found extenuating circumstances and the finding of guilt was unanimous. He ruled that at the time of the killing, Grove-Mitchell was appreciably under the influence of liquor, he was of an immature personality, there was an absence of premeditation, and there had been some measure of provocation. He was sentenced to ten years imprisonment.

I thought that was the end of a messy business, but I was not to know that Grove-Mitchell's lawyer took the case to the Appellate Division on the point of the admissibility of my evidence. The outcome of that came back to me in a very interesting manner.

Some years later, I attended a disturbance in Stamford Hill where a man had been trying to injure a dog that was barking at him through the fence. I found the man in a back alley and on searching him found a large commando type dagger with jagged edges. The man had been drinking, was being very difficult and was giving me a hard time. He was not prepared to see the error of his ways and I decided to arrest him for possession of a dangerous weapon. I suspected that the man was a Walter Mitty character who should not be let loose with the dagger.

I went through the process of giving him his rights and took him to the local charge office. In those days, the offence of possession of a dangerous weapon was not defined by the weapon itself, but by the circumstances under which it was found and the likely purpose for its possession. The accused would have been able to pay an admission of guilt fine to avoid appearing in court and the item would be confiscated to the state.

I expected that this would be the last that I would hear about the matter. I was therefore surprised to get a subpoena to attend court to give evidence in the matter a few weeks later. I got to court and saw the accused who was his usual cocky self and that he had a lawyer to argue his case.

I recognised the lawyer who had a reputation for being a devious but successful lawyer. I had seen him at work in court before where he would talk to prosecution witnesses before the case started, to try to lull a witness into a sense of comfort before delivering telling questions in court based on the information he had gleaned informally. Running true to form the lawyer came to me and began to ask about the case in a very friendly manner. I did not respond to his questions and I said that I was surprised that the man did not pay the fine and avoid the court appearance. The lawyer replied that the man did not wish to lose the dagger and therefore hoped and expected to be found not guilty and to be able to keep the weapon. The lawyer kept fishing, and it would have seemed to an observer as if we were having two parallel and unconnected conversations.

I then asked if his ability with the Afrikaans language had improved. I had seen him cross examining an Afrikaans speaking witness in English when the Magistrate instructed him to cross examine the witness in the language of his evidence in chief. The lawyer had complained that he was learning the language but was still struggling and was then allowed to use the official court interpreter. He thought that I was going to give evidence in Afrikaans, and that he was going to be at a major disadvantage. He began to flatter me and say that my English was very good. He pleaded that if I gave my evidence in English, he would keep his questions simple. He was trying to set me up, but I thought that he should have the surprise.

I was called into the witness box, took the oath and began to relate what happened. I told the magistrate that I found the man in an alley and on searching him, found the dagger which I indicated was on a table in front of the court. I related that I told him his rights and said that the accused then gave me an explanation for the possession of the weapon. I did not say what the explanation was. The lawyer immediately wrote this down on note paper and waited for me to finish my evidence before he could cross examine me. He began with some gentle questions to which I answered directly. He soon ran out of things to ask as it was a fairly simple matter. I could see that he wanted to ask me what the "explanation" was that his client offered me.

I was mindful of the Grove-Mitchell case and I did not want to just blurt it out. I wanted the lawyer to ask me a direct question. I knew that not all accused are totally honest with their lawyer, and this would put the lawyer at a disadvantage. He could not produce anything that would have counted in his client's favour, so he eventually had to ask me about the "explanation". He first broached the matter rather delicately by saying, "You stated in your evidence that my client gave you an explanation for his possession of the weapon". I replied, "I read him his rights and he gave me an explanation." The lawyer turned to the magistrate and complained that I had not answered the question. I said that I had answered the question, and the magistrate agreed with me. The lawyer was now forced to ask, "What explanation did my client give you?" I replied that the accused had told me that when the dog barked and gave him a fright, he decided to go home and get his dagger to stab the dog.

This admission had established the criteria of the "purpose and intent" of the dangerous weapon. The lawyer realised that it was all over for his client and he tried to stop me finishing. I waited for him to finish talking over me, then I turned to the magistrate and asked if I could be allowed to finish answering the question. Seeing the funny side of the lawyer being caught out at his own game, the magistrate told the lawyer that he had to let me respond to his question. The lawyer then asked the magistrate for a brief adjournment to discuss this "new information" with his client. After much whispering between an angry lawyer and a stupid client, the defence announced that it had no further questions and would only argue on the basis of the admissibility of my evidence. He was not prepared to take the chance of putting his client in the witness box to give his version of events and be cross examined by the prosecutor which would have been very enter-taining.

The prosecutor argued that my evidence was admissible because of the recently tested case in the Appellate Division of the Supreme Court of the State versus Patrick Grove-Mitchell on the admissibility of an admission made to a policeman after having been warned of his rights in terms of the Judges' Rules. In addi-tion, I had merely responded to a direct question from the defence lawyer. After a short adjournment the magistrate found the accused guilty and imposed a fine which was double the admis-sion of guilt rate. He further ruled that the weapon was confis-cated to the State. The lawyer did not hang around to have a friendly discussion about the case with me after the ruling.

———

A little after midnight on a Sunday in December 1974, I was directed to go to a home in Redhill near Durban North to respond to a report from the Durban North Fire Station of a shooting. On my arrival I was met by a fireman waiting at an ambulance at the front gate to the house. He told me that a man had driven to the Fire Station saying that they should come quickly to his home as his wife had been shot. They had followed him home and seen the body of a woman with a gunshot wound to her head. They confirmed that she was dead and called Police Radio Control to attend the crime scene. At that time the Ambulance Service was run by the Durban Fire Department on behalf of the Provincial Administration. The firemen were trained first aiders and some years later, the Provincial Administration created a separate Ambulance Service with paramedics and doctors, and much more specialised medical equipment.

I went into the house where another fireman was standing next to a man who was distraught. I saw a young woman lying on her back, and her face was covered in blood with a bullet wound above her right eye. I confirmed that she was dead. I asked the man with the fireman to identify himself and the woman. He said that he was Michael Russell-Rockliff and the deceased woman was his wife, Maureen, aged 27. I asked what had happened and Russell-Rockliff said there had been an accident. I took that to mean that no one outside the home was responsible for the shooting and I suspected that the man had shot his wife.

I was conscious that anything said or happened after that would have an impact on a court case and I immediately cautioned Russell-Rockliff in terms of the Judges' Rules and informed him of his rights. Failure to caution a suspect could render anything said by an accused as inadmissible as evidence in court. I asked where the weapon was, and the suspect handed me a small calibre pistol. I told him that I would take him to the Durban North Police Station. My intention was to take him there and arrange for the detectives to take over the crime scene to carry out an assessment which in today's forensic world would have been very basic. I told the firemen to remain at the scene with the body until the detectives arrived.

I put Russell-Rockliff in the squad car and drove to the police station. On the way he became very remorseful and asked me for the gun so he could do away with himself. I told him that it would not help things and he then explained that he did not mean to shoot her. He said that he was dancing with her holding the pistol to her head as some sort of sexual or romantic love play when the gun went off. I thought that to be a crazy response and I did not expect any court to believe that sort of explanation. That sort of sex play was not heard of in South Africa in those days and if it was true would require a lot of background information to sound convincing. The suspect smelt of alcohol, but it was difficult to assess his condition because he was overwrought, and I did not know his capacity for drinking.

I detained him at the police station and the Charge Office Sergeant contacted the standby detective to attend to the scene. I was contacted by the detectives to provide a statement and some months later I received a subpoena to attend court in a prepara-tory examination on a charge of murder. I attended court, gave my evidence and listened to the evidence of the other witnesses. The fireman at the Fire Station related that Russell-Rockliff arrived there a little after midnight and asked them to send an ambulance as his wife had been shot. The fireman then asked for particulars and Russell-Rockliff swore at him saying that his wife was more important than particulars.

An interesting turn was the evidence of the victim's brother who had last seen his sister about a month before the shooting when she complained about marital conditions in the home. Whilst this was interesting and may have possibly been an indication of the relationship or a motive for the shooting, there were no witnesses to events immediately before or to the actual shooting. Evidence was heard from the District Surgeon that a blood sample taken at 11h00 the next morning had a blood alcohol content of 0.03 and that it was probable that 12 hours earlier it would have been equal to 15 metric tots of alcohol.

The case was adjourned to a later date with the accused remaining on bail until a decision was made to charge Russell-Rockliff for murder or culpable homicide (manslaughter). I was not required for court again and I suspect that he pleaded guilty to the lesser charge of culpable homicide. It was always going to be difficult to prove a case of murder notwithstanding the testimony of the victim's brother on the state of the marriage as there were no witnesses, and the blood alcohol level and his sobriety would make it hard to prove intent to kill. Having dealt with the case of Grove-Mitchell's shooting of his girlfriend some six or seven months earlier, I could not help but wonder if he did not swallow large quantities of alcohol after the shooting to claim that he was too drunk to know what he was doing.

———

Looking back on cases after many years I can recall a handful of cases where I regret that I was not able to do more.

Umhlanga Rocks Drive ran from Durban North near the Bell Inn Pub in a northerly direction along the Umhlanga Ridge towards the present day Gateway Shopping Centre. The area around the Gateway Centre now has upmarket gated condominium villages but in 1975 the area up to Sagewood Way had houses on both sides of the road, and beyond that the land was under miles and miles of sugar cane.

One afternoon shift around 5pm, I heard the Durban North van call Radio Control and report that they had attended a complaint near Sagewood Way and needed a dog and Handler to assist in looking for a suspect that had run into the sugar cane. On my arrival I was met by two constables and an African woman who had reported an incident. The woman said that she and a friend had finished work nearby and were walking towards a bus stop to go home. They had reached the area where the sugar cane fields started when an African man ran out of the cane, produced a knife and grabbed the other African woman and dragged her into the cane. The witness had run into a nearby house and asked the resident to phone the police. The Durban North van driver arrived and looked at a sea of cane about six foot high stretching away into the distance and immediately called for a dog.

I asked the witness where the man and the woman had entered the cane, but she was so overwhelmed and shocked that she was not entirely sure and pointed in a general area. The sugar cane fields had rows of cane planted about a metre apart with a fire break every couple of hundred metres so I got one of the constables to keep an eye along Umhlanga Rocks Drive in case the man or woman exited the cane along the road, and the second constable was positioned looking down a firebreak row a little wider than a tractor.

I took Bruno to the general area pointed out by the witness and got him to look for spoor scent along the rows of cane, but he could not find the point of entry. Sugar cane is notoriously difficult to track in. The close packed and tall cane plants shut in scent and my best chance of finding anyone was to find the point of entry as the suspects and woman's scent would brush off on the cane plants and provide a track to follow. If the track was only one row away, it was unlikely that a scent in the next row would be picked up by the dog. I recall recovering a body in a sugar cane field previously.

146 | SQUAD CARS

There was no smell of the decaying body until the sugar cane around the body was pushed flat, and then the smell hit you.

I went into the cane with Bruno and we walked along rows hunting for a scent or visible signs that someone had gone through. Dense cane also muffles any sound other than cane gently rustling in a breeze. I went into the first fire break that was parallel to the road to see if Bruno could pick up a scent if they had crossed into another section but there was nothing. The dog's senses were the best chance we had, and I even looked for visible signs that cane plants had been pushed down by someone passing through, but to no avail. It was now getting dark and any chance we had of finding anyone was getting less likely.

By 7pm it had been fully dark for over an hour and we had found nothing. It seemed like the proverbial needle in a haystack. Why had the man dragged the woman into the cane? Did he know her and had a score to settle? Was his intention robbery or rape? Either way his actions were very brazen. Would he release her or kill her? It seemed more likely that he would release her as he had plenty of time to get away by either heading towards Durban North or Umhlanga. There was nothing more that I or the dog could do. The constable was going to take the witness to the Durban North Police Station to open a case and hand the matter over to the CID.

I went off duty at 9pm and came on duty again the following afternoon. Other Dog Unit members and the CID had continued to search the area the following morning, but nothing was found, and I heard no more of the case. Some two or three months later a detective from Durban North contacted me to report that the cane had been cut to be sent to the sugar mill, and the body of a woman had been found in the cane. The cause of death would have been difficult to ascertain due to the decomposed state of the body. Finding the suspect who killed her would have been almost impossible, just as it would be to bring that person to justice unless he told someone about it, and they passed that information on to the police.

I was annoyed and sad about it at the time and now some forty years later it is a case that I remember and feel that I failed. The Dog Handlers took finding suspects and catching criminals almost as a personal matter of determination and pride. We did not like to lose, especially when the consequences were so tragic for a victim and their family. The circumstances of a good hiding place in the cane making tracking difficult was a factor as well as that we only had an hour before it got completely dark and the actual point of entry into the cane was unknown. All perfectly good reasons but a sense of sadness still remains.

———

In my seven years in the Dog Unit, I worked extra duties over Christmas Eve and New Year's Eve down at the beachfront every year. Large crowds gathered in party mode at the hotels and restaurants and then spilt into the streets at midnight to party until the early hours. I usually worked down on the beachfront on special duties or on my regular shift and did not know what it was like to get into party mode with friends and family over Christmas or New Year

On New Year's Eve of 1975, I worked until 2am and then went home to bed for a short sleep, and then up to start morning shift at 7am. Shortly after coming on duty on 1 January, I received a call to go to a block of flats in lower Umbilo near Bartle Road and Oliver Lea Drive where a murder had been discovered in the domestic quarters. As it was pretty quiet at the time, Warrant Officer Sieg Mare' said that he would join me at the crime scene.

The servant quarters comprised a large room which had three beds for the cleaners and shower and toilet facilities. I opened the door and looked into the room which showed signs of a struggle. The beds were positioned at odd angles to one another and a small table was lying on its side. I saw an African male lying on his back on the floor with one leg raised against the bed. There was blood on the bed and on the floor around the man's chest and head. I saw what appeared to be a stab wound in the lower chest and his face was badly battered as though it had been repeatedly punched or beaten with a blunt instrument.

I came to this conclusion as the victim's face was covered in blood which had run into and settled over his closed eyes. Sieg was feeling queasy because he had celebrated a bit with his family after getting home from the beachfront, managing barely an hour's sleep before reporting for duty again. I looked carefully over the crime scene looking for any weapons or other tell-tale signs of evidence. I saw two small white objects lying on the floor near the body. I bent down to examine them more closely as did Sieg. They looked like pickled onions but had a few "strings" attached to them. I was puzzled as to what they could be, so I moved around to look at them from another angle, when realisation struck me. They were the victim's eyeballs! They had been plucked out of their sockets and had the optical nerves and veins attached. That was why I could not see the victim's eyes where the sockets had filled with congealed blood. When Sieg realised what he was looking at, he quickly left the room, went outside and threw up on the lawn, taking care not to contaminate the crime scene.

Siegs' Zulu crew advised us that the suspect was probably a traditional and tribal person who believed that a dying man retains the image of his slayer in his eyes. Traditional Zulus believe that if one looked deeply into the eyes of a dead person, you could see the identity of the person who killed him. This was probably a Zulu witchdoctor tradition used to smoke out evil spirits and find guilty parties in earlier times. Total nonsense in a modern, rational and scientific world but deeply believed by unsophisticated tribal Africans. Applying police investigation techniques in a multicultural environment does not mean thinking in a European or First World manner; you have to place yourself in the mind-set of the suspect and his victim.

Cleaning staff who lived and worked in blocks of flats were generally unsophisticated Zulus from the tribal areas, and we asked the caretaker of the flats for the details of the other workers. They would either be the suspects in the murder case or material witnesses. I followed this matter through with the Umbilo detectives sometime later who related that the deceased's co-workers had been in the room the previous evening but had returned hastily to their tribal area. Many Africans, who find themselves in trouble in the city, will return to their tribal homeland. African detectives would go to the suspect's tribal homeland and seek out the local Induna (sub-chief) who would tell them where the man was. If the suspect was not a regular criminal, he would have told his family about his trouble and would not try to avoid the police when they came looking for him. The detectives would show the family and the Induna all the required tribal respect and take the arrested man back to the Police Station in the area where the crime had occurred. The African detective would provide the Induna with information about where the man would be held and the date of trial so family could attend if they wished.

21

WALKING INTO THE UNKNOWN

I have previously related that police work can be made even more hazardous when insufficient information about a complaint is passed on to a policeman attending a scene. Sometimes this is as a result of inexperienced Radio Control staff taking the reports; sometimes proper information is not available; or is withheld by the person making the complaint. In certain instances, the lack of information can have serious consequences which will tax even the most experienced policeman.

One Saturday morning shift around midday, I received a report to go to an address in Sea View where the estranged husband of a woman was allegedly creating a disturbance. I did not know whether the woman would be there or to whom the house belonged. I was closest to the address, without a crew and no back up was available at the immediate time, but a colleague would be sent to join me when he became available. I stopped outside the house which was an old style Edwardian cottage with a front verandah. I saw that the front door was open as I walked along the pathway, then up a small flight of stairs onto the verandah, from where I saw a man in the lounge.

I walked in and greeted him in a relaxed manner. He immediately backed off to put distance between the two of us. He was on edge. I was watching his hands for sudden movements and looking into his eyes to try to see what he was up to. I tried to calm him down by saying that I was attending a report of a disturbance and asked if he could tell me what was going on. He was highly agitated, and he did not want me to get too close to him. I did not know whether he had committed any crime, so I did not want to grapple with him. I asked him where his wife was, and he replied that she was not there. I tried to get him to talk to me and put him at ease. We spent several minutes like this whilst my eyes swept the room for any signs that would help me make sense of the complaint. I saw papers on the table but could not make out what they were.

I asked him for identity or proof of residence, but he merely replied that he had none. I instinctively knew that something more serious was going on as he was not relaxing or responding to my gentle questioning. I suggested that we go outside to my car so I could take his details and report back that everything seemed in order. I wanted him out the house and I wanted to ask Control to get back to the complainant for more detailed information. I also wanted back up as I suspected that the man was going to make an impulsive move.

I managed to manoeuvre him onto the front verandah when another squad car stopped outside, and Sergeant Sparky Van Niekerk walked up the front path. I was momentarily distracted by looking at Sparky and when I looked back at the man, he was drawing a pistol from the back of his trousers, raising it and pointing it at Sparky. I lunged at his arm and grabbed it whilst trying to wrestle it away from him. Sparky ran towards us and grabbed the man around his waist from the rear. The man moved against a support column on the verandah to steady himself as we wrestled for control of the gun. He was trying to turn it alternatively on Sparky or me. It was like an arm wrestling competition where the weapon pointed in the direction of Sparky's head and then away. I tried to pull his arms down before applying pressure on his hands to release the gun. I did not want to jerk the weapon or his arm as he had his finger on the trigger and he may discharge a round.

Sparky was still behind the man hanging onto his waist having seen the barrel point at his head. Sparky ducked behind the assailant's back and said "Oh God!" several times, keeping cover behind the man without contributing much to the struggle for the gun. The man turned the gun inwards towards his chest and I managed to wrestle it away, but he again pulled it back towards himself. We were wrestling up against the verandah support column which was an awkward position so I could not get good leverage to pull the weapon away. The gun discharged and the man was shot in the chest. I felt him go limp in my arms and he looked at me as his eyes rolled and glazed over and he died almost instantly. I was wound up and said, "You stupid cunt!" which was probably the last thing that he heard in this life.

Sparky was badly rattled, but I was more annoyed that the man had been able to get the weapon out without me spotting it, and because I was unable to get the weapon away from him. I called for an ambulance and laid the man out on the verandah. I could now check the house out for some indication of what was going on. I then noticed that the front door had been forced and I found a suicide note on the table. I later found out that the dead man was a Mister Hook who had gone to the house with the intention of shooting his wife and then committing suicide. When he realised that she was not there, he wrote a suicide note and was going to shoot himself so his wife would find his body.

I submitted a statement and an inquest found that his death was as a result of suicide. I felt a little sorrow that he had died but my overwhelming feeling was one of disappointment that I had not been able to prevent him shooting himself. I was aware then as I still am today, that people make decisions about their lives, and whilst we should do as much as we can to help them, they must walk their own path.

22

TEAMWORK AND A WEAK LINK

The Durban Dog Unit was unlike anywhere else I worked in terms of team work and the support and reliance we placed on one another. We were faced with potentially dangerous encounters every time we put on our uniforms, climbed into the squad cars and went out on the streets. We had all applied to join this unit and had been selected by a switched on commander who used his senior subordinates to get feedback on the abilities and relative merits of the applicants.

There was friendly competition to be the best, and the prize was the Eric Gordon trophy. Making the most first schedule (serious crime) arrests was not something that could be exaggerated or falsely claimed as members of the shifts would often be there as backup and would know if someone was falsely claiming cases. Arrests came from attending complaints and reports by the general public as well as our own ability to seek out crime by analysing the crime hotspots from checking the station crime registers and talking with detectives.

Arrests were written up in the dog register that was accessible to all, so we knew what our colleagues had been up to and we celebrated their success. We did not feel that anyone on our shifts may just lack the edge to perform when the chips were down. We could confidently arrive at housebreakings or robberies knowing that a teammate was covering the back door or was just behind you to give you cover if needed. We would be annoyed with ourselves if we missed a suspect, or if a suspect got away from us. We set high standards and demands on ourselves and those who worked with us.

I tried to take the principles and practices of teamwork learnt in the Dog Unit with me to other roles and jobs in my later working life. I became aware that whilst teamwork was crucial when the consequences of failing were severe, other teams in other jobs had a range of people with different abilities and aims from those who wanted to be the best. Some were comfortable in the job and did a satisfactory job whilst others just plodded along because the consequences were not the same.

Teamwork in the Dog Unit was based on trust and ability. No one had to be defensive or watch their back, so their focus was on the case or the complaint without internal distraction. We could have discussions on different or better ways of doing things without having hard feelings. Commitment was key. We wanted to be there, and we knew what the standard was. In addition, we had an animal we cared for and we were not going to put the dog in a position where it may get hurt because we failed to stay close and act bravely. We accepted accountability for ourselves and our teams which included respect for each other and holding our teams to higher standards, especially by the senior ranked members. The Dog Unit had a justifiably good reputation with the public and we were determined to uphold that. We focussed attention on results, particularly with applying investigation techniques and police procedures to preserve evidence for the detectives and the law courts.

In late 1974 I was called into Major Hennie Meyer's office. He informed me that a Sergeant had been transferred to Durban from a Dog Unit elsewhere in the country. Although Meyer never gave me details of the reason for the transfer, he alluded that he had "domestic problems". I will call him Sergeant Lawrence. Major

Meyer told me that our unit was significantly more proactive and dedicated to attending serious crime in progress than other units and he wanted to place him on my shift and to keep an eye on him. He suggested that I should post him as a crew on my vehicle for a few shifts to instil the Durban ethos. Lawrence was to join the shift that evening for the night shifts.

Lawrence was about 10 or 15 years older than me and whilst we patrolled various parts of the Durban area, he told me that he had a major domestic issue that resulted in the Police Chaplain recommending a transfer to give him a fresh start elsewhere. I was trying to give him an overview of the demographics and crime trends throughout our area but he did not seem to be responsive. Around one in the morning he told me that he was tired as he had been moving into a new flat and asked if I would mind if he slept whilst I drove. Members in our unit did not sleep on duty and I suggested that we would do more active things to keep him awake. I was not impressed with him on our first meeting, but I was prepared to see how he developed.

After a week, he was posted to his own vehicle with a crew and was allocated to a patrol area. I noticed that he liked to spend time in the Indian shopping and residential area of Grey Street in the centre of town. I would hear him report that he was standing off to attend some or other disturbance in the street or at some café or food outlet. It slowly dawned on me that he would ingratiate himself with the local shop owners to get free food and big discounts on various items of clothing or other goods.

I would also hear Control asking him to attend to domestic disturbances. Dog Handlers would rarely attend domestic disturbances as we should be kept available for more serious complaints. The station vans would attend this sort of problem and we would only help if the complaint was likely to become serious or if Control could not despatch another vehicle in a reasonable time period. He would spend a significantly longer time at disturbances than other members of the unit resulting in him not being available to attend more serious cases where a dog would be useful. I questioned him on this, and he indicated that he wanted to sort things out so that we did not get recurring complaints from the same source.

Early one morning around 3am, four or five dog cars gathered in Pine Street to get coffee from the automated 24 hour coffee shop and asked Sergeant Eivind Gjosund to go to the Albany bakery in nearby Umgeni Road to buy some donuts. About 10 minutes later, Control reported a fight at the Cosmo Nightclub which was about 100 meters from the Albany Bakery. Gjosund heard this and offered to attend. Nightclub complaints could be very serious as sailors from around the world would frequent them as well as locals who were on the gangster fringe. Many nightclub complaints flared up and were sorted out fairly quickly so were often all quiet on the arrival of the police. We expected Gjosund to report back soon and then bring the donuts down to the rest of the shift working in the Central area.

Constable Siwa who was crewing with Gjosund came on the air and breathlessly asked for support because a group of men were fighting with them. We all raced off to the scene with my colleagues following a roundabout route along a one way road system. The fastest route was straight up Soldiers Way against the one way system, and this was the route that I took because there was very little traffic at the time. I was the first on the scene and as I approached, I saw that two or three men had pushed Gjosund onto the bonnet of the police car and were punching him. Siwa was wrestling with another two or three men. I did not stop to ask what was going on because policemen were being attacked and they should expect an aggressive response.

I took Bruno out and set him on the two men assaulting Gjosund. One turned towards me throwing punches. I ducked the incoming fist and let loose with punches of my own, dropping the man. I heard the other dog cars screeching to a stop as more friends of the attacking night clubbers joined in and fought with the police. It was a brawl involving eight or nine civilians and around six policemen and we all climbed in. Sergeant Boet Nel had a clash of heads with one on the night clubbers and had blood streaming down his face. We arrested all the men for disturbance and assault on police and loaded them into police vans which we called to the scene.

Thinking back and discussing the brawl with some of my colleagues a few hours later we realised that Lawrence's role in the brawl was running around picking up fallen police caps, and opening kennel doors as we pushed prisoners into empty dog kennels until the vans arrived. By now a number of my colleagues and I had doubts about his courage. I checked the dog register to analyse his arrests and found that most arrests had been handed over to him by civilian complainants rather than through his own efforts. Most of the shift realised that he stayed off the air at domestic disturbances to avoid being sent to serious crimes in progress.

I spoke to him about how few serious cases he was attending compared to other members of the shift and he denied that it meant anything. Other shift members could not recall him arriving at a crime scene when they would still be chasing or looking for suspects. He seemed to arrive when everything was under control. By now the other members on the shift did not want to work with him as they did not feel comfortable having him as a backup in any serious incident.

A few weeks later, Flip Sonnekus was complaining to me about Lawrence. The Radio Station Indoor Supervisor on my shift was my old friend Gert Van Den Berg formerly from Stamford Hill. I explained my suspicions about Lawrence and suggested a test. Gert made a routine request to all the dog cars to report their present positions. This was done by the shift Warrant Officer from time to time to ensure that the entire region was covered so that most areas could be reached with little delay. We asked two or three of the Dog Handlers to phone me at Radio HQ, where I told them not to offer to attend a crime in progress that would soon be reported. They then contacted Control over the air and stood down at stations to undertake some or other work.

Lawrence had earlier said that he was in Umbilo, so Control tasked him to attend a non-existent housebreaking in progress at a corner shop in the Umbilo area. He replied that he could not attend and asked if anyone was closer. He was informed by Gert that no one else was available and he would have to attend immediately. He replied that he was going to the Cato Manor offices and could not attend. He was driving away from the affected area. He was then instructed by Gert to attend but again said that he could not. I then came on the air and Gert reported that Lawrence would not attend a housebreaking in progress. I instructed him to attend and he replied that he had to go to Cato Manor urgently. When I insisted and wanted to know why he could not attend, he responded that he needed to go to the toilet urgently.

In the end he did not attend, and we knew for certain that he was a weak link in what needed to be a strong chain. The story went around that the thought of having to attend a crime in progress made Lawrence shit himself. We were stuck with a lame duck and no one had any confidence in him. I would have to manage him closely which was challenging when you are in separate cars miles apart, with other productive members of the team requiring back up and support.

Some months later, Lawrence was injured in a vehicle accident whilst off duty. His injury made him unfit for further active duty. He was posted to Radio Control indoor staff and out of the Dog Unit on return to duty after an extended period of sick leave.

23

COUNTER INSURGENCY COURSE

E arly in 1975 I was informed by Lieutenant Chowles that I was in a group of about 5 Durban Dog Handlers who had been nominated to attend a 2 month counterinsurgency course in Pretoria before deploying to the Rhodesian border area (now Zimbabwe) for a 4 month tour of duty. I had no problem with this as I had attended a 4 week course in 1970 and missed several previous deployments for various reasons, and besides, I could hardly be regarded as one of the top members of the Unit without having done at least one tour of border duty. The SAP had been deploying policemen to work side by side with the Rhodesian Police and Army in the North Eastern border area of Rhodesia close to the Mozambique border since 1966/7.

The Rhodesian border area had been hotting up with an increase in terror incidents against white farms and the local population, plus there had been a recent attack against a South African Police patrol. A patrol of 6 policemen armed with assault rifles had developed the habit of leaving a camp in the Rhodesian border area, following the same route to a spot in the river where they would strip off and swim. They probably started by keeping a watch of a couple of armed men whilst the others swam in the heat of the day, but they became complacent and would all swim without any armed cover. They had been observed by a group of terrorists who caught them in the water, held them up and then beat them for information before shooting them all dead. It may have been partly in response to this incident that a large number of Dog Handlers and their dogs were to be deployed to accompany patrols to seek out terrorists and avoid ambushes.

The background to my call up to deploy to Rhodesia was to be affected by a complex and changing International political situation. The right wing Salazar regime in Portugal which had been in power for nearly forty years was overthrown in a military coup in 1974. Salazar had maintained the colonies in Mozambique and Angola by fighting the nationalist liberation or terrorist groups that were agitating for independence. Young Portuguese men were compelled to do national service against these groups and the national will to maintain the colonies was diminishing.

The interim government in Portugal was engaging with these movements in Africa to hand over sovereignty. This naturally gave impetus to the liberation movements in Rhodesia and South Africa. The Zimbabwe African National Liberation Army (ZANLA) was operating from Mozambique and they stepped up their activities in Rhodesia.

Further developments took place whilst I was undergoing the training. South African Prime Minister John Vorster had made a trip to Liberia in February in a bid to open a dialogue with Africa. On 10 March, we heard that the SAP units in Rhodesia had been confined to their camps and active patrols had ceased; whilst in South Africa, Braam Fischer, the former head of the South African Communist party had been released from gaol on compassionate grounds as he was dying from cancer.

On 18 March, Herbert Chitepo, a senior ZANLA Commander was killed in a car bomb in Lusaka, Zambia. There was much speculation about who was behind it. The initial view was that he was killed by Rhodesian or South African agents, but a later view was that he was killed because of an internal power struggle, with Robert Mugabe benefitting most from the incident.

*Durban Dog Handlers on Bush Course February & March 1975: L
to R: Sid Brettell, Ronnie Muller, Nickie Fourie & Eivind Gjosund.
Nickie Fourie later joined the Afrikaner Weerstands Beweeging
(AWB) and was shot dead in the Bophuthatswana uprising in
1994*

I drove up to Pretoria in my Chev Kommando around the end
of January or early February so I would have transport for weekends. I would also be able to make the odd trip home on a
weekend before Bruno and I flew out to Rhodesia. The course was
a mixture of weapons, tactics and special dog training focussing
on tracking to adapt to a rural counterinsurgency role.

We went to a farm for a week, where we lived in tents and prac-
ticed tracking and ambush drills. The farm had none of the usual
agricultural activities and was left wild to resemble areas of mixed
bush, hilly outcrops and veld, fairly similar to areas we expected to
operate in. We were split into two groups with one group required
to follow spoor and search and find the other group which was to
attempt to set up an ambush. The ambush group had to avoid
being seen or smelt out by the dogs of the other group. I was in the
ambush group and we selected an area of bush that was slightly
raised and gave a view of the veld dotted with thorn bushes. Most
importantly, we were upwind of the direction from which we
expected the attacking group to come.

We spread out on the edge of the bush and waited for the
second group to enter into our field of fire. We were in a good
ambush position and we expected that the other group would be
well spread out with a number of the dogs in the forward position

to guard against being surprised in an ambush. We intended to let any forward trackers enter or skirt past the bush so we could have an effective ambush of the bulk of the approaching group. We had seen some game on the farm but mostly from a distance. We did not expect any dangerous predators to be on the farm other than snakes. After a couple of hours, we saw a number of small antelope moving towards us looking in the direction of the approaching group. That was our indicator that they were on their way and were heading in our direction.

River crossing on Counter insurgency course

The small antelope skirted past the bush and we expected the hunting group to come into sight at any time. Suddenly a group of five or six large gemsbok came into view at a run and came straight at us hiding in the bush. Gemsbok are large antelope that are 1.2 metres high at the shoulder, and males can weigh between 180 to 240 kilograms with spectacular straight horns up to 80 cm long. I slid across behind a tree and dragged Bruno with me. We all lay flat and kept our heads low. A fleeing gemsbok almost ran over Ronnie Muller, only becoming aware of him as he stepped right next to him. The gemsbok instantly dipped his horns in reaction and Ronnie missed being gored by inches. The instructors who were following up saw what happened and the ambush was called off. We had to regroup and play ambush again the following day. Our choice of an ambush site was good and demonstrated the bush craft required for counter insurgency operations. Many of us who had spent time in the bush or in the Boy Scouts and being in the Dog Unit knew our way around.

About six weeks into the training, the newspapers reported ongoing high level discussions between the South African government and Britain and America who were seeking ways to reduce the conflict in Rhodesia. South African Prime Minister Vorster met Zambian President Kenneth Kaunda in a train on the Victoria Falls Bridge to support internal solutions with Rhodesian African nationalist groups and the Rhodesian government. A week later, Dog School announced that only about 10 or 12 of the 30 Dog Handlers under training would deploy because of the changing situation. One would think that it would have been a hard decision to work out who should go, but there were a number of men who insisted that they go because their wives had already bought new household appliances in the expectation of increased allowances relating to the deployment.

The smaller group was deployed to bases on the Rhodesian border area but were withdrawn after several weeks. The South African Government decided to withdraw its Police Counter Insurgency Units from Rhodesia to allow the internal and external liberation factions and the Smith Government to reach a peaceful solution to governing and running Rhodesia. The ongoing infiltration of guerrilla forces continued with the mainly Ndebele tribe ZIPRA (Zimbabwe People's Revolutionary Army) operating out of Zambia supported by the Russians whilst the mainly Shona tribe ZANLA (Zimbabwe African National Liberation Army) operated out of Mozambique supported by the Chinese as unrest and incidents escalated.

24

THE PRIEST AND THE BOY

One night a little after midnight, I heard Sergeant Mervin Van Rensburg report that he was chasing a vehicle near the Rugby Stadium and a few minutes later a breathless Mervin came on the air and asked me to meet him in Umgeni Road. On my arrival I saw a small car with two wheels on the pavement facing the wrong direction of travel. The rims seemed to have hit the pavement side-on and the tyres were flat. A middle aged White man wearing a long black priest's frock was sitting on the pavement looking very sorry for himself whilst Mervin was seething with annoyance when he related what had transpired.

Mervin reported that he went down a dark backstreet near the Archery Club fields where we often went to let the dogs run and relieve themselves. He had seen the small car parked up on the grass verge which seemed very suspicious as there was nothing down that road. Mervin thought that it may be an abandoned stolen car or possibly a couple making out. The windows were steamed up, so he went up to the car and shone his torch which lead to a flurry of activity in the front seats as two people quickly moved apart. Mervin related that it looked as though the person in the driver's seat had his head in the groin area of the other person.

He ordered them to open the door and to his surprise he saw that the occupants were an adult White male and a very young teenage African male who was trying to get his erect penis tucked back into his trousers.

The Immorality Act was passed in the mid 1950s which dealt with a wide range of sexual offences relating to under aged sex and people who lacked the mental capacity to consent but was primarily remembered for the ban on sex with persons of another race. In the 1960s tabloid type newspapers would report on stories about pillars of Afrikaans society in small towns being caught having sex with African maids and prostitutes. This had elements of scandal and serious stigma which caused some people to commit suicide. By the mid to late 1970s sex across the racial barrier was seen as petty Apartheid and rarely resulted in prosecutions unless it contained other aspects of illegal sexual activity. Same gender sexual acts were still offences at that time.

Mervin took the teenager, put him in the back of the police car and then turned his attention to the adult. His opening line was to ask the man what his wife would say when she was told what he was up to. That would usually lead to shock and begging not to tell anyone. The man was very cool however and said that he was not married. Mervin asked him where he worked and lived, and he responded by saying that he was a Catholic priest who lived at the Cathedral in Durban Central.

This surprised and annoyed Mervin who told the man to wait at the car while he walked a few paces away to his squad car to ask questions of the teenager. The teenager was a homeless street child who was probably picked up in town. Mervin was trying to get more information when the priest jumped in his car and raced off. Mervin followed in hot pursuit. It was an uneven battle and the Priest lost control of the car as he tried to go around a corner at high speed. He slewed the car into the pavement and came to a stop. Still in a state of panic he tried to run away. Mervin stopped the squad car and pulled out his pistol calling on the priest to stop but rather than using a standard "Stop or I'll shoot", he called out "Stop you cock-sucking priest or I will blow your f***** head off!"

The priest stopped, and Mervin ran after him still in a state of excitement, and hit the priest dropping him to the pavement.

Both parties had lost their composure but Mervin, realising what he had done, called me because I was the Shift Warrant Officer and would know what to do and also because I was a Catholic. Mervin related the story to me in front of the priest, and I asked the priest if the story was true. He admitted almost every detail but was reluctant to discuss what happened in the front seat of the car. I took Mervin aside and asked him if he could be absolutely sure of what he saw, and if it would stand up in court. Mervin realised that cross examination about the dew and frosted windows would be attacked by a good lawyer. I told Mervin if he was sure of what he saw, he should decide if he wanted to charge the two, but he did not feel too comfortable about that.

I went to the priest and asked how he would explain the situation if I took him to see Archbishop Hurley. The priest equally did not want to go through that and he was unlikely to report that Mervin assaulted him. Mervin arranged for the car to be removed and I took the priest back to the Cathedral telling him that he should do some soul searching and make a full confession as I would be in touch with the Bishop the next day. That incident was overtaken by a range of other issues and I went home to sleep and never got on to the Bishop.

Recent revelations about priests and abuse of vulnerable boys and attempts by the Catholic Church and other churches to conceal child abuse by priests and ministers over the past 30 years is a very sorry period for religion. Naively at the time, I had no idea that abuse of that nature was going on. I am sorry, in hindsight, that I did not go and see the Bishop, whatever the outcome. The best solution would have been for me to take the priest and the teenager to the Cathedral and asked to see the Bishop, relate what had happened and ask what they were going to do about it. I did however tell Mervin that it would be unwise to hit a priest again, especially if I was close, in case a lightning bolt was despatched to strike him.

25
_____

NEW THREATS AND NEW RESPONSES

The 1972 Munich Olympic massacre of Israeli athletes shocked the world and introduced a new form of terrorism to parts of the world that previously felt safe. The taking of hostages with the making of demands and shooting of hostages presented Police with problems they had not expected or been trained to deal with. The ambush and rescue attempt failed, and a number of the hostages were killed.

The shootout with the well-trained Black September terrorists showed a serious lack of preparation on the part of the German authorities. They had not expected to have to deal with this sort of situation. Policemen were called upon to be snipers, a role that they were not adequately trained or equipped for. This costly lesson led directly to the founding of police counter-terrorism branch GSG 9. Many other countries had to review their specialist resources and update the training and equipment issued to their personnel.

To my knowledge, the South African Police and other authorities did not take any special measures to address a similar threat. Most of the Arab world had instituted sanctions and boycotts of South Africa so the likelihood of Arab terrorists even getting into the country was highly unlikely. Police had riot training that may have stood up to a mob group of strikers and riot shields and batons were available in stores at Wentworth on the Bluff but nothing capable of dealing with something of the magnitude and complexity of what happened in Munich. That all changed in late April 1975.

On 28 April 1975 around 1pm, a local newspaper in Johannesburg received a phone call from someone inside the Israeli Consulate in Fox Street, Johannesburg saying that it had been taken over by three Lebanese and three Japanese terrorists, and the staff were being held hostage in the building. The Israeli Embassy was opposite the Carlton Centre right in the heart of the business district.

Soldiers and police, together with government ministers and senior officials, converged on the area. As the police and military were deploying, they were sprayed with machine gun fire from the fifth floor embassy. The police and soldiers returned fire. The event made world news as the Israeli cabinet went into emergency session. The siege continued as a stalemate all day when the South African Prime Minister John Vorster, broadcast to the nation that evening that he would never negotiate with terrorists under any circumstances. This position was echoed by Israeli officials in Tel Aviv.

Contact was set up with the hostage takers in the Embassy and the police were informed that over twenty employees and some of their children inside the building had been handcuffed and wired with hand grenades and explosives. Negotiators were able to establish that two hostages in the embassy had been shot and tried to get the terrorists to agree to have a doctor tend to the wounded. Using a walkie talkie radio, it was agreed that they could send a doctor stripped to his underpants into the embassy to treat the wounded. An army medic, Dr Gottlieb entered the building and reported when he came out that two consulate officials were wounded. Both men later died. The pregnant wife of one of the shot officials was allowed to leave.

The doctor was able to reveal that this was only a one man

operation with no Lebanese or Japanese terrorists involved at all. The pieces of the story were coming together. The hostage taker was 24 year old South African Jew, David Protter, who was employed as a security officer in the embassy. He was discharged from the Israeli Army three years earlier as unfit for service as he was mentally disturbed having impersonated an Israeli Paratroop Captain. He'd been arrested and served time in gaol before being deported back to South Africa. His record was not known by the embassy staff when they engaged him as a security officer as a thorough security check was not carried out.

Protter had gone into the embassy early on the morning of the 28th before any other personnel and began taking hostages as they reported for work. He reportedly told them that there was a security drill and took them into a steel sided reception room whilst he kept them covered with a machine gun. It was puzzling how even a heavily armed man could accomplish this whilst being vastly outnumbered. The presence of children may have limited any resistance.

Negotiators were able to get Protter to release hostages in batches early on the morning of the 29th and at around 6am he gave himself up. The shooting rampage resulted in four deaths and some forty injuries to bystanders. There was some confusion whether all the injuries and the death of one of the officials in the embassy was caused by Protter, or return fire by the police and military.

Protter pleaded guilty to all charges including the counts of murder and was sentenced to 59 years in prison. Surprisingly, after serving only 16 years of his sentence, Protter was released unconditionally in 1991.

This event required a rethink on responses and preparedness to terrorist incidents in South Africa. A Police Reaction Unit was established with a training regime that included entry and rescues in aircraft, abseiling down buildings, sniper training and specialist weapons, following tactics used in countries that had already faced terror incidents. This had a knock on effect for members of the Durban Dog Unit. We were required to go to Radio Control at the start of each shift to collect a shot gun and a R1 SLR rifle with extra ammunition which we wrapped in blankets and locked in the boot of the squad car. If a serious incident arose, we could contain the situation with extra firepower until the specialist Reaction Unit was deployed.

26

CHASING STOLEN CARS

C hasing stolen cars was a hazardous activity for the policemen in pursuit, the driver and passengers in the stolen car and other road users. Criminals usually had little regard for anyone else as they focussed almost solely on escaping. People stole cars for a number of reasons ranging from organised criminals who wanted a car to use in robberies, to modify and sell on, or to cut up for spare parts. There were even isolated cases of stealing a car just to get home. The people who stole cars also had a wide range of driving abilities, from being a very competent driver, to others who were erratic and could not handle a car at speed, often resulting in them losing control and spinning out with minimal damage, or crashing spectacularly.

Policemen at the time were less concerned about recovering the vehicle intact than getting the criminals off the streets. We wanted to bring the chase to an end as quickly as possible to minimise collateral damage to the public. Experience had shown that once you arrested a driver of a stolen car, objects in the car or the driver and passengers' fingerprints often connected them to other cases. Many car chases were not identified as stolen cars when they first came under suspicion. Seeing a vehicle being driven erratically could be a drunken driver, or a stolen car driven by someone who was unfamiliar with the gears or steering. Once a suspicious vehicle was spotted, the squad car would ask Radio Control to check the registration number against a card index of reported stolen cars. The control staff would come back as quickly as possible with a positive or negative response. The squad car would either call for back up or if unavailable, race up alongside the vehicle and indicate to the driver to pull over, and get a little ahead, ready to cut the car off to bring it to a stop. It did not however always work out that way.

Around 2 am in September 1974, Constable Badenhorst was driving the van from the Greenwood Park Police Station when he observed a Mini 1275 GT car on North Coast Road that was weaving from side to side. Suspecting that the driver was drunk, he tried to stop the vehicle, but it sped off heading towards town. The Mini had great acceleration with a relatively powerful engine for its light body and a low suspension that gave it terrific cornering ability. The vehicle registration was checked with Radio Control who confirmed that the car had been reported stolen earlier that evening in Umbilo.

The stolen car headed from North Coast Road into Umgeni Road with Badenhorst in hot pursuit. Control called vehicles near the centre of town to intercept the Mini. A road block was set up in Umgeni Road opposite the Cosmo Night Club, with two station vans pulled up sideways across the road, with two dog cars and the Duty Officer's car just behind. We saw the Mini coming into view around a corner and the driver would have had 100 metres to stop before encountering the police vehicles drawn across the lanes of travel. The stolen car driver had other ideas and mounted the pavement at a driveway access to a shop, sped along the pavement and around the police vans then made a sharp right turn into Alice Street.

The squad cars took off after him and could gain on the Mini on the straight. I drew next to the Mini and swerved sideways towards it in an attempt to get it to pull over. To my surprise, the driver swerved back at me almost attempting to push me off the road. The chase continued into Old Dutch Road heading towards the Berea. I drew alongside the Mini and pointed my revolver at the driver. The sight of the revolver diverted his attention long enough for him not to see a dividing island where the road split off to the left down Wills Road. The Mini hit the island at speed and became airborne for about 3 metres, remaining upright, hitting the pavement and then a wall at the entrance to a block of flats before coming to a stop.

I ran up to the car and grabbed the driver who was remarkably unhurt. To my surprise, he was a youngster who said he was thirteen years old. He may have lied about his age to see if that got him off a charge, but he was definitely not older than fifteen or sixteen. I placed the suspect in the back of the Umbilo van when I saw something glint in the streetlights at the first floor landing at the top of the stairs of the flats. I went up the stairs to investigate and found one of the hubcaps of the Mini lying there. The force of the impact had shocked the hubcap off and propelled it up a flight of stairs which showed how lucky the youngster was not to have been seriously hurt. The youngster was detained at a Place of Safety and appeared in court the following day.

Even when a policeman has had many years of experience in dealing with crime and criminals it is not possible to say you have seen it all. There is always the possibility that something may surprise you, and this was no exception. The youngster had shown some driving skills and quick reactions to avoid the road block, and was not overawed by the larger squad cars drawing up alongside him.

———

Amanzimtoti, 25 kilometres south of the Durban Central Business district, had good bathing beaches and lagoons that attracted holiday makers who wanted a restful time away from the busy Durban beaches. The area was mostly residential and had many hotels and holiday flats along the beachfront with the population more than doubling during the school holidays. The South Coast highway ran a further 130 kilometres south beyond Port Shepstone to the Wild Coast and the boundary of the Natal Province. The area south of Amanzimtoti was a mix of natural coastal bush, sugar cane and banana farms, with little villages popular with pensioners dotted every few miles down the national road.

Around 12.30 am in October 1974, Constable Du Plessis of Amanzimtoti was patrolling the national road when he saw a car speed past him heading South. He gave chase advising Radio Control that he was in pursuit of a suspected stolen vehicle. The registration number was checked and was confirmed as stolen. I was assigned to the Durban South area and was informed about the chase. I headed for the highway and picked up speed as the Chevrolet Kommando's 4.1 litre engine powered me down a virtually empty road, reaching speeds in excess of one hundred and sixty kilometres an hour.

Du Plessis was managing to stay with the stolen car and as he was approaching Scottburgh about 30 kilometres south of Amanzimtoti, the stolen car screeched to a stop and three African men jumped out and ran into the bush. Du Plessis stopped the van and ran after them firing a number of shots as they disappeared in the dark bush. The suspects probably expected that the police at Scottburgh or Umkomaas further south had been contacted and would be waiting for them a little way down the road. I arrived at the scene about 10 or 15 minutes later, grabbed my powerful six battery torch and took Bruno out the kennel.

Du Plessis indicated where the men had run into the bush. It could have been confusing for Bruno as Du Plessis and his crew had also mixed their scent with the suspects at the point of entry into the bush. It was a positive that the scent was no more than fifteen minutes old and no one else was likely to be in the bush. When tracking a spoor, we would usually put the dog on a 30 foot puppy line made of light weight rope to keep the dog in close proximity. I decided not to use the puppy line as it would have got tangled in the bush, so I chose to jog along behind Bruno as he followed scent. In the light of the torch, I could see how the bush had been trodden down so it was relatively easy to follow a visual spoor as well as the dog.

The moon was close to full which gave sufficient light to make out larger bushes and trees. Bruno followed the spoor in the bush for a couple of hundred metres and then came out at a footpath. He would drop his nose to the ground from time to time as he jogged forward with me about ten paces behind. The scent was strong so we could move forward at a good pace. Bruno stopped and then ran off the path a little way into the bush. He sniffed around and came out and continued down the path in the general direction of the sea. I concluded that a suspect had probably been hiding in the bush at the point that Bruno entered, but had decided to move on if he heard us approaching. I thought that we may be gaining on them as Bruno picked up the pace before running off the path and into the bush. Bruno started to bark about 10 meters into the bush as I ran after him. He had grabbed hold of a man who I arrested and handcuffed. The man was sweating profusely so he clearly was not someone who was simply sleeping in the bush.

I brought the suspect back to the van and handed him over to Du Plessis before going back to the bush. We searched for other scent, but Bruno did not indicate other spoor in the general area. I concluded that the suspects had split up and if they were in the vicinity when Bruno found their mate, they would have put as much distance as possible between them and me. I was informed by the detectives at Amanzimtoti some days later that the suspect I arrested had his fingerprints found in the stolen car and they were hopeful that they could either get him to tell who his accomplices were, or to see if he had previous convictions in the company of others who would be his likely mates.

Du Plessis and Radio Control had the presence of mind to realise that the stolen car chase would result in the suspects abandoning the vehicle and running off into a sparsely populated area ideal for tracking. My Dog Unit colleagues and I had instances where policemen had run all over a spoor area, and much later as a last resort when their efforts had failed had only then called for a dog, which usually failed to provide positive results.

Around 2.30 am in 1975 Sergeant Mervin Van Rensburg with his dog Nero and Constable Len Hutton with his dog Wagter were patrolling in a southerly direction on Sydney Road near the Union Flour Mills. They noticed a car travelling in the opposite direction without lights. As the car went past them they noticed two men in the car. They immediately executed a U turn to follow the car whilst asking Radio Control to check the registration.

The car noticed the squad car turn to follow and they accelerated reaching speeds of 130 Kilometres an hour. Radio Control reported that the car had been stolen a few hours earlier so the policemen would do their best to bring the car to stop as quickly as possible. There was little traffic on the roads so the policemen tried to come alongside the stolen car and force them to pull over. The policemen could see that the driver had no intention of stopping so Len Hutton leaned out the window and fired shots at the tyres of the stolen car.

The shots missed and instead of the driver of the stolen car deciding to pull over and surrender, they drove even faster and more erratically. The two cars were now approaching West Street some four kilometres from where they spotted the stolen car. The stolen car entered an intersection a high speed but failed to see that a section of road was under construction and drums had closed off the road works lanes. The stolen car hit the drums, slewed across the road and hit a light pole coming to a stop. The policemen stopped with the knowledge that car thieves would run off like Olympic trialists and they had to get their dogs out quickly before they disappeared into the alleys near the market.

The passenger was first out and off running with Hutton and Wagter after him. The driver's door swung open and Van Rensburg released Nero expecting to see the driver streak off down the road. The driver was quite a bit slower and took only a few steps before Nero latched onto his calf. Van Rensburg was surprised that the driver was not shouting or reacting to being bitten by the dog as he ran towards them. Van Rensburg got to Nero and took him off the driver who was amazingly calm and quiet for someone who had just been tackled by a police dog. Van Rensburg handcuffed the driver as Hutton returned to the squad car with his prisoner who had been tackled by Wagter.

The two policemen then inspected the suspects for weapons and injuries. Van Rensburg lifted the driver's torn trouser leg to see if he had any puncture wounds that required medical attention and was surprised to see that Nero had been biting on a wooden prosthetic lower leg. That explained why the driver was not as good a runner as his companion and why he was so calm when the dog had caught him.

In January 1979 around 2 am, Constable Frans Gunter was patrolling in his dog car near the Tollgate Bridge when he spotted a Mini heading out of town with two men in the vehicle. The men looked apprehensively at him when they drove past him. Gunter followed asking Radio Control to check the registration number. Control confirmed that the car had been stolen. Gunter very sensibly asked other vehicles to give him back up before he tried to stop the vehicle as it had slowed down to about eighty kilometres an hour hoping that the policeman was not going to take any action.

I was close so I offered to join him when Constable Bartie said he and his dog were also close behind. The freeway had very little traffic at that hour, so we raced to catch up to Gunter and the stolen car reaching speeds around 200 kilometres an hour. As we approached Gunter and the stolen Mini, I said I would drive past the Mini and pull in front of him, whilst Gunter would pull alongside, with Bartie bringing up the rear to box them in. I shot past and pulled in front of the Mini and slowed very quickly. The driver of the stolen car accelerated and shot past me almost clipping the rear of my car. We were approaching the off ramp of the freeway which would lead into the Old Main Road in Pinetown.

The off ramp swung sharply to the right over Paradise Valley with sheer drops down to bush in the valley below. Negotiating the turn required vehicles to slow down but the Mini went into the turn at full speed drifting across the two traffic lanes hitting the left side concrete and metal barrier that was all that stood between them and a twenty metre drop to the valley floor. I braked sharply and saw the passenger who was not wearing a seat belt fly into the back seat on impact with the barrier. The crash into the left side barrier was a glancing blow that catapulted the car across the lanes for a second collision, this time with the right hand crash barrier. This second impact caused the passenger to fly out the rear window which also popped out on impact, whilst the driver fell out the now shattered driver's door and landed on the road surface.

I stopped my squad car as the two men leaped up and ran off towards the end of the off ramp about one hundred metres distant. I called on them to stop and released Bruno. Both men showed no effects from the collisions and were sprinting as Bruno narrowed the gap. Bruno targeted the man closest to him, who on seeing the dog about to grab him, promptly and without looking jumped off the bridge. I could hear Bartie and Gunter coming up behind me as Bruno turned his attention to the remaining suspect who on seeing that Bruno was about to grab him also jumped off the bridge. I thought that they must have done some serious injuries to themselves as I ran on to the end of the bridge, scrambled down a steep embankment towards the valley floor and found a 2.4 metre fence blocking my way.

I struggled to lift Bruno above my head, but he helped by pulling himself up with his front paws and leapt over the fence whilst I followed as fast as I could. I heard Bruno barking as I moved through the dark using my torch and diffused lights from the freeway. I found one of the men who had suffered a broken arm which was very lucky considering the injuries he could have sustained. I brought the suspect out as Bartie helped his dog over the fence to look for the second suspect which they found hiding in the bush with minor injuries.

The two suspects could not have been familiar with the Paradise Valley area and the drop to the valley floor. If they had known that they could have been killed, they might have chosen to stop and give up. I came to the conclusion that many criminals do not always think through the various scenarios that they may be faced with when they commit crime. The absence of a Plan B and being faced with arrest usually leads to a mad panic and running off into the unknown with unusual consequences.

That was not the only action that night. Around 4.30 am just before dawn, the Umbilo Police van spotted a stolen car in Oliver Lea Drive near Carrington Heights and when he tried to pull the car over the driver raced off down the winding road at high speed. He called for backup, but a number of the dog cars were standing off at complaints or police stations with arrests. In the absence of other squad cars, I offered to help, but I was near Point Road. The shortest and most direct route was not the quickest, so I raced along the Esplanade which had the Durban Bay on my left with no traffic coming from that direction, so there was only possible traffic from my right at intersections. I took the Southern Freeway which took me past Oliver Lea Drive, but I would get there quickly since I was travelling at speed with no intersections. I heard the van driver report that the car had lost control on a bend and had left the road, ending up in the Umbilo Canal near the intersection with Umbilo Road.

I stopped the squad car near the van and looked into the canal which fortunately had little water in it. The canal usually only ran with water after heavy rain in the hills around Carrington Heights. I saw the constable at the vehicle which surprisingly had remained on its wheels when it plunged into the canal. He called to me that the man had locked himself in the car and was refusing to unlock the doors and come out. Bruno and I climbed down to the car in the canal. The driver was sitting in the driver's seat with a smug look on his face. I tapped on the window and told him to open the door, but he sat there doing nothing. He then took out his cigarettes and lit one, casually smoking and ignoring us.

I told the constable to force the vent window on the passenger side to get his hand in to lift up the lock. He did so but when he put his hand into the car, the suspect produced a plank of wood and repeatedly wacked his hand. The pain made him pull his hand out, so I then forced the vent window in the driver's window, and we tried to reach in for the lock on both sides simultaneously. The suspect began to whack us in turn, but we were determined and managed to pull the locks up. I thought, "You SOB. We are going to get you!"

The suspect then began a pulling contest as we tried to pull the doors open. He could not hold both doors closed at the same time, so whilst he was whacking me the constable reached the lock and pulled the door open. Bruno was aware of what was going on and was running from one side of the car to the other. When the constable got his door open Bruno jumped in like a flash and grabbed the man by his sleeve and began jerking him around. The man jumped into the back seat to get away from the dog and tried to open the door to get out, but those doors were still locked. Bruno jumped into the back seat area and the previously cool character had lost it as the rough and tumble, growling and snarling got his attention. I could not miss the irony that he would not open up and now when he wanted to get out, he couldn't. I opened the front door, got into the driver's seat and called Bruno off. I asked the driver if he still wanted to stay in the car with the dog or if he wanted to go with the constable. The funny man asked to go with the constable. Both the constable and I had bruises and broken skin on our hands and arms, but it was worth it to see the expression on the suspect's face change from smug to panic.

———

Looking back after many years it seems that most car chases resulted when police intuition told us that things did not look right, and the thief's guilty nerves gave them away before the car was reported stolen. Car chases seemed to take place shortly after the car was stolen when the thief's adrenalin was high, yet after they had fitted false number plates they would try to stay cool and bluff it out. Thieves in a stolen car with false plates were less inclined to panic when they saw a police vehicle but when signalled to pull over, they would realise the game was up and take off at high speed.

There were fewer motor cycle chases than car chases probably because there were much fewer motor cycles in use in those days. School boys who turned sixteen could get a licence to ride a 50 cc "buzz bike" which they often used for school and getting around, but they seemed to aspire to get a car once they could afford one.

In March 1978 I had come on duty for the night shift and had spent some time with the Radio Control indoor staff reviewing the afternoon incidents and reports. Around 10pm, I decided to go to the Dog Unit offices at Cato Manor. I had just gone past the Mayville Police Station approaching Manor Gardens when I saw two men on motor cycles in a side street with the one fiddling with the engine. The Manor Gardens area leading to Cato Manor was undeveloped with open plots of land and apart from a few houses and shops near the Dog Unit offices there was little else in the area.

I stopped the car and reversed back to the men and the bikes, but they took off riding past me at high speed. I had spooked them and their guilty behaviour of speeding off made me think that the bikes had been stolen. This feeling was strengthened when I saw that one of the bikes had no lights and the driver did not have a helmet. The other bike had lights on and the rider had a helmet. I chased them down the road reaching speeds of 120 kilometres an hour as we approached the intersection with Francois Road. At the intersection the riders split up with one heading left and the bike with no lights taking a right turn towards Cato Manor. I decided to stay with the bike with no lights. As we approached Bellair Road, the rider missed his gears as he prepared to take a tight turn. I had to stop the bike before he got onto the long straights of Bellair Road and picked up speed increasing the likelihood of him crashing and injuring himself. I realised that it was now or never.

I knew that the corner had grass verges, so I drew alongside the bike and crowded him onto the verge. He lost control of the bike and fell off, but he jumped up like a shot and ran down the road. I stopped the squad car quickly, ran after him and caught him after a short chase. I checked that the rider, a young man in his early twenties was unhurt and then looked at the bike. The ignition had been tampered with, so it appeared to have been stolen. I asked for a police vehicle to get the registration and owner details from the licencing office so we could confirm that the bike was stolen. The young man had heard my instructions to get the registration details, so I gave him the standard warning that I was arresting him on suspicion of theft and asked him if he wanted to tell me anything.

The suspect claimed that the other rider had asked him to help him collect a bike and only when he got to a house in Manor Gardens did he realise that he was helping him steal the bike. I asked him who his accomplice was, and he offered to take me to the large Old Mutual Towers flats in Pinetown. I got a Dog Handler and his crew to join me and we took the suspect to the flats. We parked the squad cars a distance away from the flats in case the other suspect was looking out for us and then decided to look around the flats' car park for the other motor cycle. Our suspect was keen to help, and he pointed out the bike his mate had ridden. We arranged for that registration to be checked before we went up to the second suspect's flat.

We told our suspect that we would knock on the flat door and if the occupant asked who was there, he should answer so we did not have to break the door if he refused to open up. The occupant opened when he heard his mate's voice and the shock on his face when he saw the police uniforms was priceless. We took him down to the car park area and brought the squad cars closer to get feedback on the ownership of the motor cycles. The owner of the bike stolen from Manor Gardens had been contacted and we established that the second bike was also stolen and fitted with false licence plates.

Both men were taken into custody and I handed the case over to the Dog Handler who accompanied me. The two suspects pleaded guilty in court with the first suspect getting a suspended sentence, and the second and main accused getting a short jail sentence.

27

UNCERTAIN TIMES

S outh Africa in the 1960s and 70s were uncertain times. I was a young child when the Sharpeville massacre occurred in March 1960 when after a day of demonstrations against pass laws, a crowd of about 5,000 to 7,000 protesters went to the police station. The South African Police opened fire on the crowd, killing 69 people and injuring 180 others. Sources disagree as to the behaviour of the crowd. Some reports state that the crowd was peaceful, while others state that the crowd had been hurling stones at the police, and that the shooting started when the crowd started advancing toward the fence around the police station. There were 249 casualties in total, including 29 children.

In present day South Africa, 21 March is celebrated as a public holiday in honour of human rights and to commemorate the Sharpeville massacre.

I remember my parents discussing the massacre and its implications. My mother was involved in canvassing to retain the Union in the 1960 referendum which led to South Africa leaving the Commonwealth and becoming a Republic.

Momentous events were also taking place in countries to the North that would impact on stability and peace in South Africa.

The Belgian Congo became independent in June 1960 and the following month an army revolt broke out with violence spilling over to the civilian population. Belgium sent troops to protect fleeing European colonists. Katanga and South Kasai seceded, allegedly with Belgian support. Amid continuing unrest and violence, the United Nations deployed peacekeepers, but Secretary General Dag Hammarskjöld refused to use these troops to help the central government fight the secessionists. Congo Prime Minister Patrice Lumumba responded by getting assistance from Russia in the form of military advisors, equipment and logistics.

The arrival of the Russians led to friction in the Congo government and Lumumba was overthrown and killed. The multi tribal Congo disintegrated, with various factions establishing militias that fought to expand their territory as European settlers fled the country. Unrest continued into 1964 with massacres and hostage taking of missionaries and settlers. A rebel group surrounded the remaining European population in Stanleyville, gathering them together and holding them in a hotel, using them as bargaining chips. Belgian paratroopers supported by American aircraft landed in a rescue attempt and liberated the hostages but around seventy hostages and a thousand civilians died in the rescue. White mercenary groups were established to put down the rebellions and the central government under Mobutu slowly established order.

At the end of 1964 the Federation of Rhodesia and Nyasaland was dissolved with Northern Rhodesia becoming the independent Republic of Zambia, whilst Nyasaland became the independent Republic of Malawi. Southern Rhodesia remained a colony but after failed negotiations with Britain, declared unilateral independence in November 1965. African liberation movements in Rhodesia then engaged in increasingly active insurgency tactics including attacks on white farms and security forces, and politicisation of the local people.

Also on South Africa's border were the Portuguese colonies of Mozambique, with Angola to the north of the South African mandate of South West Africa. Portugal had maintained colonies for hundreds of years with many Portuguese nationals living and working there in commerce and industry. The winds of change in Africa with many of the former European colonies getting independence in the late 1960's and early 1970's resulted in calls for independence, and the rise of liberation movements in the Portuguese colonies.

Notwithstanding the Portuguese colonial wars of counter insurgency, Mozambique and Angola experienced economic growth in agricultural products, minerals, fishing and textiles. The wars were placing greater financial demands on the Portuguese economy and men were conscripted to do military service in the colonies whilst women were rapidly incorporated into the labour market. By the early 1970s the Portuguese military was overstretched with no political solution in sight. Morale of the troops deteriorated.

Whilst the casualties remained relatively low there was no political solution in sight and international pressure made them feel increasingly isolated. Thousands of young men avoided conscription by immigrating to other countries, primarily France and the United States. In April 1974 there was a military coup in Lisbon that overthrew the government, and a decision was made to withdraw from their African colonies. The coup was relatively bloodless and is referred to as the Carnation Revolution.

The liberation movement in Mozambique, the Front for the Liberation of Mozambique (FRELIMO) was actively expanding its influence in the rural and tribal areas whilst the Portuguese army controlled the towns and populated areas. The Portuguese government began talks with FRELIMO and handed over power to them in June 1975. Portuguese colonials in the country areas moved to Lourenco Marques (now Maputo) to avoid fighting and the 250,000 colonials waited to see what would happen next. The FRELIMO government ordered the Portuguese to leave the country with 24 hours' notice and only 20 kilograms of luggage. Unable to salvage any of their assets, most of them returned to Portugal penniless.

Former Portuguese colonials who lived in Lourenco Marques

and settled in South Africa told me that the order took them by surprise and they only heard about it when they saw Portuguese officials heading to airports and the harbour, leaving the settlers with little information or guidance. Many colonials loaded up their cars and vans and headed to South Africa where a number went into settlements hastily set up by the South African government. Others headed on to Durban to get a ship back to Portugal. South Africa had a relatively large population of Portuguese speakers living in the major cities who took many of the refugees into their homes. Many stayed on in South Africa. The Durban dock area was crowded with Mozambique registered cars, with refugees looking to get their cars and goods back to Portugal. Some six months later I still saw many older Mozambique registered cars abandoned down side streets as it became apparent that the fee for shipping a car was greater that the value of the car.

Angola was even more confusing. There were three rival liberation movements competing for power with their power base drawn from different tribal and geographic areas, as well as influence from various competing powers in the Cold War. As the Portuguese left Angola a war between the liberation movements started with advisors from the Cold War powers using proxy troops to further their interests. South Africa was drawn into the conflict as the African National Congress (ANC) sided with the Marxist MPLA and it was feared that Angola would become a safe haven for the ANC and SWAPO (The South West African People Organisation) to undermine the South African mandate in South West Africa.

Further North, Idi Amin, the President of Uganda who had taken over the government in a coup, accused the country's Indian community of disloyalty, non-integration and commercial malpractices; claims the community denied. In 1972 Amin declared that Britain would need to take on responsibility for British subjects of Asian origin, accusing them of sabotaging Uganda's economy and encouraging corruption. Amin defended the expulsion by arguing that he was giving Uganda back to ethnic Ugandans. Nearly 30,000 British Asians moved to the UK, and thousands of other Ugandan Asians relocated elsewhere in the world. Asians owned many large businesses, but the expulsion affected every area of Uganda's economy with most of the businesses going to the state.

The Cold War was very active in Africa with powers jockeying for position and influence. China was building a railway running from Zambia to a port in Tanzania.

These events would add to the political isolation of South Africa and strengthen the boycotts and sanctions movements. I felt it was my duty as a policeman to protect and serve everyone against this background of uncertainty and expectation.

28

SPRINGFIELD TIN TOWN FLOODS

The Durban Dog Unit was called upon for many varied things outside their usual police mandate. If the public did not know what to do they would ask a policeman, and Radio Control received some funny requests. It is probably good that the public contacted the police if they did not know what to do as it indicated a level of confidence that the police would sort it out. The South African Police motto was "Servimus et Servamus" meaning to Serve and Protect so that was a catch-all, to serve and protect the public of greater Durban, no matter the issue.

The Umgeni River rises in the Drakensberg Mountains and runs for two hundred and thirty kilometres to the sea at Blue Lagoon about two kilometres north of the Durban harbour. The river has a number of bridges crossing over to Durban North, and towns and farms up the North Coast of Natal. About two kilometres inland from the river mouth at a large bend in the river is the Springfield flats where Indian market gardeners had established themselves almost 100 years earlier. The market gardeners had built homes of corrugated iron and wood at their plots, and by March 1976 there were just under 500 occupied "tin houses". The residents provided vegetable produce to stores and markets in Durban.

March in Durban starts to cool a little after the oppressive heat of February with temperatures reaching the upper twenties and an average rainfall in March of 130 millimetres or a little over 5 inches. Heavy rains would cause the level of the Umgeni River to rise, threatening some of the houses built on low lying land.

In 1917 after heavy rain there was a major flood when debris that had built up around the base supports of bridges upstream broke free and a wall of water flooded across Tin Town washing houses and people downstream towards the river mouth. At that time, a group of six Indian sein netters in their boat rescued scores of people, but sadly over a hundred people lost their lives.

On 20 March 1976, Durban and the area upstream had heavy rain, making the river rise and flood its banks, and flow into the Tin Town settlement. Members of the local police stations and the Dog Unit arrived on the scene, after being alerted by the public. The Durban Fire Department and the Durban City Police were alerted, and they combined to rescue many of the residents, with particular attention to the elderly, the infirm and the young. Members of the Dog Unit took off their tunics and pistols and went into the waist high water, helping the community to get to higher ground, as well as remove household and personal articles to safety.

Once the residents had been safely evacuated, they turned their attention to pets that had been stranded on shack roofs, and some dogs that were chained and left treading water. Constable Doug Linden and Sergeant Nicky Kleynhans were photographed picking up and carrying man's best friends to safety. The Dog Unit members remained on the scene until they were satisfied that all residents and animals had been moved to safety, and the Council services were making arrangements to account for and shelter the residents. When the Dog Handlers got home their wives and girl-friends would have seen by their appearance that it was an unusual shift with large batches of muddy and dirty washing.

Whilst the residents had lost their livelihood, homes and contents, there were no reported fatalities.

The City Council took over the relief efforts of the community and a tent town sprung up at the nearby Asherville Sports Grounds. The flood was reported to have washed away 222 shacks on the lower lying area of the settlement. The Mayor of Durban, Dixie Adams, established the Durban Flood Relief Fund with an initial fifty thousand rand and the public donated generously. The Flood Relief Fund committee comprised local community leaders and activists including Fatima Meer, JN Reddy and Amichand Rajbansi amongst others. The Council undertook to give the evacuees priority housing in the Phoenix Township that was being established.

Constable Doug Linden and Sergeant Nicky Kleynhans rescue dogs from the Tin Town floods

29

SOWETO UPRISING

E arly in June 1976, I applied for four weeks leave to study for promotion exams to Lieutenant. I had to cram six subjects in that brief period as shift work and attending court on days off made getting into the syllabus ahead of time a challenge. On the evening of 16 June, I heard a news report on the radio that students in Soweto had rioted, buildings had been burnt, and police had opened fire with a number of students killed and injured. Scenes were shown on television, and the newspapers the following day had articles and photos that sent shock waves through South Africa as riots and damage spread to other African townships with heavy handed police responses.

The background to the riots were ascribed to the use of Afrikaans as a medium of education in African schools. Some two years earlier the Regional Director for Bantu Education issued a decree that African schools should use a 50/50 mix of English and Afrikaans as the medium of education. The instruction was deeply resented by Black students with Bishop Tutu referring to Afrikaans as the language of the oppressor. The African Teachers Association of South Africa objected to the decree to no avail. Resentment grew until in April 1976, pupils of the Orlando West

Junior School refused to attend school, and the momentum spread to other schools in Soweto.

A student from Morris Isaacson High School, Tsietsi Mashinini, proposed a meeting on 13 June 1976 to discuss what should be done. Students formed an Action Committee later known as the Soweto Students' Representative Council, which organised a mass rally for 16 June, to make themselves heard. The students marched to the Orlando Stadium. A group was stopped by the police with a dog which was killed by the students, and the police opened fire on the group. The violence escalated with bottle stores and beerhalls being looted and set alight, as were other sites that were regarded as symbols of the apartheid state.

An initial estimate of the number of students killed in Soweto was twenty three, as well as two white people working in the area, including Dr Melville Edelstein who was employed by the West Rand Administration Board. He had devoted his life to social welfare and disability among blacks and was stoned to death by the mob and left with a sign around his neck proclaiming "Beware Afrikaners".

Violence died down by nightfall as police reinforcements patrolled the area. Emergency clinics were set up to treat the injured. The following day large numbers of police were deployed with a detachment of the military in reserve to prevent a repeat of the violence. Crowd control methods used by South African police at the time included mainly dispersal techniques. White students from the University of the Witwatersrand University marched through Johannesburg in protests. The University of Zululand's records and administration buildings were set ablaze, and 33 people died in incidents in Port Elizabeth in August. In Cape Town 92 people died between August and September.

The Soweto riots as they were called then, caused economic uncertainty, and the Rand fell against other currencies. The United Nations passed a resolution condemning the South African government and international pressure increased.

A number of student leaders fearing arrest made their way to other countries joining the ANC in various roles including propaganda and training as guerrillas.

By the time I had written my exams and returned to work things had quietened down in the Durban area with sporadic protests and outbreaks of violence in various parts of the country. I felt very unsettled. I had married at the beginning of the year and had a baby on the way. I had been hopeful that politicians and the peoples of South Africa could find a way to address realistic aspirations, ensure economic progress and mutual respect. My hopes for a better society, and my contribution to safety and security had been dimmed and I did not see a way forward, but like most others, I would do my best and look for the positive.

30

BUSY NIGHT SHIFTS

For those policemen who wanted to prevent crime and catch criminals, night shift was the time where squad cars and dogs' capabilities could be best used. Morning shifts were quieter, so half the shift would go off into the Cato Manor bush to train the dogs and practice tracking and "bark out" searches for suspects hidden in the bush or in buildings. Afternoon shifts would get busier from after six when the public got home from work or went out for sport or entertainment. The night shift started at nine and ran through to seven the following morning. The busiest time would often be around shift change for night shift and Dog Handlers were always keen to wrap up a complaint before 9 pm to get back to Cato Manor, put the dog in the kennels and get the mini bus transport home.

The weather impacted on the incidence of crime. If it was raining heavily, we could expect less crime because not only would criminals be put off by the rain but there would be fewer people moving around in the rain so they would stand out. The summer had higher incidence of crime. The hot weather seemed to make people more inclined to violence, so assaults and robbery with violence increased. It would start getting light from around

4.30 am at the height of summer so criminals who had been active during the hours of darkness would move down to transport hubs early in the morning to get away with their stolen goods.

Weather would affect burglar alarm call outs too. High wind would rattle windows and doors where contact alarms were fitted, resulting in a high incidence of false alarms. By the mid 1970's alarm systems were becoming increasingly more sophisticated and effective, and many businesses were installing them to protect their properties. The owner of a burglar alarm system could decide if they would come out to check a report of an activated alarm or pay for the alarm company to attend on their behalf. The alarm company would have a set of keys to open the premises when the police arrived. We generally found that the alarm company keyholder was more efficient as they got to the premises quicker and they were familiar with working with dog and Handler, which meant less waiting time for us.

A good example of a busy night shift was when Sergeant John Rabie and Constable Mervin Van Rensburg were working together as driver and crew with both dogs in the same squad car. Fairly early in the evening they received a report of an alarm and on arrival covered the premises until the keyholder arrived. They released one of the dogs into the shop and the dog barked out a suspect who had hidden himself when he heard the police arrive. The man was arrested and taken to the police station and placed in custody whilst the policemen submitted a statement on the arrest.

They returned to the vehicle and advised Control that they were back on the air and available for complaints. Shortly there-after they were asked to attend another alarm which also resulted in an arrest. The suspect was taken to the local police station and detained. After completing the paper work, they booked back on the air and were asked to go to a butcher shop where an alarm had been triggered. On their arrival they found that a large quantity of meat had been removed from the fridges and had been repacked in boxes for removal. The butcher shop owner came out in response to the alarm and on gaining entry the Handlers and dogs arrested a suspect in the premises who was taken into custody.

The two policemen were about to drive off when the rather happy butcher stopped them and gave them each a meaty bone for their dogs, which was gratefully accepted. The two policemen were feeling rather pleased with themselves as they had attended three complaints and made arrests at all three cases, and the dogs had been given a meaty reward from a grateful complainant. The dogs were given the bones and were happily chewing away in the kennels behind the Handlers as they drove off.

By then it was the early hours of the morning and they continued to patrol, waiting for Control to direct them to the next complaint. A short while later they spotted two men carrying heavy bundles. Two men coming out of the dark needed looking into, as they suspected that they were in possession of stolen property. They stopped next to the men who immediately dropped their bundles and ran off at speed. Both policemen jumped out and opened their respective kennel doors to release their dogs after the fleeing men. The policemen then proceeded to run off after the suspects expecting to see the dogs run past them. After a few paces they realised that the dogs had remained in the kennels, and the fleeing men had disappeared down the road and out of sight.

The dogs had continued to chew on their bones. They had decided to take a canine version of industrial action and refused to follow orders. The policemen later saw the funny side but may have had mixed feelings at the time, since the bundles were found to contain items that had been taken in a housebreaking.

———

Late in January 1977 I reported for a Saturday night shift at 9 pm, paraded the shift and assigned members to their patrol area. Sergeant Jan Storm who was on the afternoon shift was delayed with a complaint so the mini bus took the afternoon shift home and I waited for him. Once he put his dog in kennels, I offered to take him to his home in Pinetown. We were about two blocks away from Storm's house travelling down a minor residential street when we saw two men walking towards us carrying heavy bags. They spotted the car at the same time we saw them. They dropped the bags and ran off in the opposite direction.

I called after them and released Bruno who streaked after them. Bruno tackled the first man and was hanging onto his sleeve. I quickly grabbed the man, released Bruno, and sent him after the second man. The second man saw that the dog was about to catch him, so he stopped, and Bruno held him until Storm got to him. Bruno had a good temperament and knew that someone in uniform was part of our team. Many of my crews were comfortable in holding him, and on a few occasions released him out the kennel if I was caught up with someone else. Most of the suspects he tackled had no injuries as he would grab clothing, unless they resisted or hit and kicked out at him.

We brought the two men back to the squad car and then examined the contents of the bags. They contained clothing and other household goods and appeared to have come from a housebreaking in the vicinity. We later established that a house in the nearby Birdhurst Road had been broken into and goods taken. I arranged for the Pinetown Police Station van to pick up the suspects and stolen goods and I dropped Jan off at home. That felt like a good start to the night shift; a crime solved with suspects arrested and goods recovered before the homeowners even knew about it.

As I was in the western part of Durban, I decided to patrol the area to familiarise myself better with the roads and suburbs. Pinetown was the largest town to the west of Durban at that time. It had a large and busy commercial centre with apartment buildings and housing sprawling out from the town centre. The road to Johannesburg ran through Pinetown and rose up Fields Hill towards the villages of Kloof and Hillcrest.

Kloof was a leafy upper class suburb in what is known as the mist belt with roads winding along the ridge, and large houses in sizable tree-filled grounds. Kloof means gorge in Afrikaans, as the

Molweni Stream had created a deep gorge, a large part of which was included in the four and a half square kilometre Krantzkloof Nature Reserve. The Krantzkloof Reserve was home to mammals such as duiker, bushbuck, mongoose, Cape genet and caracal, with a large variety of birdlife including crowned eagles and peregrine falcons. Many of the houses had magnificent views across the gorge, and privacy and space between houses gave a real "out in the country" feel to the area. Beyond the gorge lay Zulu tribal lands that stretched away in the distance in an area known as the Valley of a Thousand Hills.

Sometime after midnight, Radio Control called for vehicles in the Kloof area as a burglar alarm had been received from the Kloof Cottage Tearoom in the Maytime Stores Centre in Village Road. I was close by and said I would respond. Two other dog cars would follow as back up. We all knew of recent events at Maytime Stores. There had been a number of break ins at the shops in the centre, and alarm systems had been upgraded. The criminals had often smashed windows, taken valuable items and left quickly before the police arrived. Maytime Stores had hired a night watchman to augment the alarms as a deterrent to further break ins. The night watchman had been murdered some months earlier and security companies had declined to assign staff to the centre. We knew that we would probably face some determined and ruthless housebreakers.

I told my colleagues that I was going to park the squad car some distance away from the Centre and approach on foot with Bruno. I knew that two cars were minutes behind me. I approached the Centre and stood in the shadows. Maytime Stores had a small row of parking spaces outside the five or six shops that made up the complex. There were no cars outside the shops, and I saw no movement outside the shops. I approached the Kloof Cottage Tearoom cautiously, which was the first shop in the row. I heard hammering coming from the shop and saw that a window had been forced. The windows had been reinforced with burglar guards and I saw that the burglar guard had been forced back and bent inwards with a gap just wide enough to squeeze through. The window was opposite an office in the corner of the store, with a deli counter and shelves away to my right. The shop lights were on and I could see two men in the office hammering a chisel into the top of a safe door.

I looked around and saw a colleague approaching with his dog, so I went to the window and lifted Bruno up to get in. I was close enough to cover Bruno if the men were armed. As Bruno went through the window, the men looked up and saw me and the dog. I had to squeeze through the window and bend and push the burglar guard away to get in. One of the men ran out the office and into the store. I temporarily lost sight of him as Bruno went after him. As I got through, I saw the second man in the office jump up on a desk and pull himself through an open hatch into the ceiling. I saw a pistol on the desk, and I realised that the stakes had been raised. I reasoned that if they had firearms, they would not hesitate to use them. That made me all the more determined to arrest them not just for this offence but other crimes we were sure to link them to. I thought that if they got away they would be free to commit other serious crime with firearms, and we would have to face the victims.

My first priority was to get to Bruno. I took a few paces into the store and I saw that the first man was on the floor struggling with Bruno. There was a large smear of blood on the floor and my first thought was "Bastard! He has stabbed my dog." My next thoughts were that we were not going to let these guys get away. I went to help Bruno overpower the man on the ground and quickly cuffed him. I then heard the man moving in the ceiling, with the sounds heading towards the rear of the shop and a probable escape route. I shouted out to him to stop and fired a single shot in the general direction of the sounds in the ceiling. I heard a shout and the man then fell through the ceiling, landing on the floor of the shop.

My colleagues helped me handcuff the second suspect and check him for injuries. He said his backside was burning and there was blood on the seat of his pants. We took his pants down and found that he had been hit right between his butt cheeks. I turned my attention to Bruno to check for injuries and was relieved to find that he was not injured. Bruno had gone after the fleeing first suspect as he ran into the store and grabbed him by his ankle, causing him to fall and hit his head on the corner of a fridge, sustaining a cut that was the source of the blood I saw on the floor.

We went into the office and found that the safe door had been partly opened with a chisel and screwdriver still stuck in the gap of the door. I inspected the pistol and found that it was a very good replica, but not a real firearm. We found a number of carrier bags filled with goods ready for removal. High value, low weight, and easily sold items which usually included cigarettes, and the till had been ransacked. The Hillcrest Police van came to the scene and the local detectives arrived to follow up on the break in. The two suspects were removed for medical treatment which confirmed that their injuries were not serious. The Duty Officer attended the scene as I had discharged my firearm and he had to satisfy himself that I had acted within the law.

The criminals were caught because they were greedy! They saw a safe and thought that it contained large amounts of money that they could get out before police arrived. The detectives informed me some weeks later that they were able to link the suspects to a number of robberies and housebreakings in the area, but they could not find any links with the murder of the watchmen. I believe that the murder would be closed as "undetected" some several months later.

————

The Natal Mercury featured a colour photo of me and Bruno on the front page in the Monday paper, with a more detailed article about the arrests on page 3. The paper had recently started using occasional colour photos on the front page as photos previously had always been in black and white. I looked at the photo with a mixture of satisfaction and a little embarrassment by the importance shown to the event, but I rationalised it by thinking that it was good publicity for the Dog Unit in general and added to the public's confidence in the police.

A FORMIDABLE team — Warrant Officer Syd Brettell and his faithful dog Bruno, of the Durban Police Dog Squad. They have been responsible for scores of arrests and many criminals behind bars can bear testimony to their savage and determination in fighting crime.

31
___

THE STANDER GANG

I n 1977, Sergeant Vince Zimmerman, his dog and crew were patrolling along the M4 in a northerly direction near Durban North. The M4 was the main North Coast route running from the Umgeni River to Umhlanga and beyond. It was mid-morning and traffic was light. Zimmerman became aware of a car approaching from the opposite direction on the other side of a wide grassed traffic island. The car was travelling faster than other traffic but not excessively, so he was able to see that the driver was a white male with a beard and long hair. The image he saw was not entirely out of place, but his instinct triggered, and he decided to follow the car; something just felt out of place. He had to drive on to a traffic glide off and underpass to get onto the Durban bound lane to follow the car. He picked up speed when the radio in the police car reported a bank robbery in nearby Glenashley by a single white male with a beard and long hair followed by a description of the car. It was the car he saw a minute earlier. He accelerated and after crossing the Umgeni River and being faced with many road options in town, realised that he had lost the vehicle.

Banks and Building Society branches in South Africa in the

mid 1970's were mostly open plan, with tellers sitting at desks so as to be accessible to their customers. Security was light and there may have been a security guard outside the bank keeping an eye on customers as they approached the door.

In this case the robber had entered a Glenashley bank branch and approached a teller in a confident and friendly manner, produced a gun and a bag, and told her to fill it with cash. The frightened teller handed him the bag and he got up, calmly left the bank and drove off in a car. The car was later found to be from a car hire company at the Durban airport.

The robber was thirty one year old Captain Andre Stander of the Kempton Park Detectives. He had reported for duty that morning, briefed his team and assigned duties and then caught the hour long flight to Durban where he put on a wig with a false beard and moustache, hired a car at the airport and drove to Glenashley to rob the bank. He then removed his disguise and left the car at the airport and caught a flight back to Johannesburg in time to put in an afternoon's work with his fellow detectives. This was the first of many robberies by him over the next three years.

Stander's father was a senior police officer who encouraged his son to join the police and he advanced rapidly to become an officer in the Detective Branch. At the time of the Glenashley robbery, his father was the Major General in charge of the Police Dog School and his advance may have been thanks to his family connections. Stander may have found his job boring; his marriage was troubled, and he clearly lacked a moral compass. For the next three years he operated alone, making one change to the planning of his first robbery. He realised that hiring a car was risky, so he took to stealing a car to commit the robbery, and he continued to operate in Durban as it was far enough away to make him an unlikely suspect, yet close enough for a quick flight to Durban and back to Johannesburg.

It was estimated that in a three year period he stole in the region of one hundred thousand rand (R100 000). By comparison, my salary as a new Lieutenant in 1977 was in the region of six thousand rand (R6 000) a year, and I bought a four bedroom house the following year for twenty six thousand rand (R26 0000).

Stander needed to launder his money, so he and a friend bought a souvenir shop in Durban. He was successful because he knew what the police responses would be, but he was contemptuous of them and their ability to catch him. He kept his secret to himself until late 1979 when he had too much to drink and confided in his friend and business partner about the excitement of robbing banks and asked his friend to join him. His friend did not believe him so to really get his point across he told his friend that he had a stolen car parked at the Johannesburg airport. When his friend would have no part of it, Stander passed it off as a joke.

The friend was troubled and discussed the incident with a senior police officer who undertook a search for the car at the airport car park. The car was found, and an internal search discovered a balaclava, a number of wigs, false beard and false number plates in the boot. The items were left in the car which was placed under observation. Early in January 1980, Stander was observed removing items from the car, and the following day a bank was robbed in Durban. The police were waiting for Stander when he arrived back in Johannesburg and he was arrested in the arrivals area of the airport. He had four thousand rand (R4000), a balaclava, a revolver, and a false moustache and beard in his luggage.

Stander faced 28 counts of robbery in the Durban Supreme Court, was found guilty of 15 counts and sentenced to 75 years imprisonment; an effective 17 years as the counts ran concurrently. He claimed that he had been brutalised during the Soweto riots and had shot unarmed students, but it was proven that he was not involved in any police actions at that time.

At the Zonderwater Maximum Prison, Stander met other hard core criminals and formed a relationship with Patrick McCall, a bank robber and car thief, and Alan Heyl who was convicted on bank robbery charges. They plotted to take any advantage to escape prison and concocted a story in which they claimed to have injuries that needed special treatment outside the jail. In August 1983, Stander and McCall together with other prisoners and 3 armed guards were taken out of prison to see a physiotherapist at a private clinic. Stander and McCall jumped the guards, disarmed them, took the physiotherapist's car keys and drove off. They knew that the car was hot, and they were still in prison clothing so they drove down a nearby farm road and held up a farmer, instructing him to phone the local police station to report a relatively minor problem.

A solitary policeman arrived at the farm and Stander and McCall held him up, with Stander getting into his uniform. They locked the farmer and the policeman in the back of the police van whilst McCall changed into some of the farmer's clothing. They drove off in the police van which they stopped on a nearby secluded road and flagged down a passing car. They locked the driver of the car into the back of the police van together with the policeman and the farmer, before leaving in the car. The policemen and the others in the back of the van eventually kicked out the window at the rear of the cab and escaped, but by the time they contacted the police, Stander and McCall were far away.

Stander and McCall went into hiding, living quietly for two months. Stander was a brazen man though who knew that his friend, Heyl, was due to write a trade test at a private centre under supervision of armed guards. Stander and McCall ran into the centre with guns drawn, held up the warders and examiners, and released Heyl before driving off in a high powered car. A few days later the trio raided a gun shop in Randburg, shooting and wounding the owner before removing a number of heavy calibre weapons and large amounts of ammunition.

The gang then went on a robbing spree. Between November 1983 and January 1984 they robbed over 20 banks with a haul of over half a million rand. They were so confident and brazen that one day they robbed three banks in quick succession, in the same area, in under an hour. There was no running into banks with guns drawn or racing get away cars. They were relaxed, confident and well dressed, and did not fit what was thought to be the typical bank robber appearance. The men were however pushing their luck, and they realised it as there had been some narrow escapes. The trio decided to go overseas so they decided to buy a yacht. They started to negotiate to buy the Lily Rose in Cape Town docks.

In late January, the three robbers were photographed by a video camera during a bank robbery, and the high quality recent photos were circulated in the media. A few days later, Stander flew to Florida in the USA on a false passport with the intention of selling the Lily Rose there. Meanwhile in South Africa, the police received a tip off that led them to a safe house used by the gang in the upmarket suburb of Houghton in Johannesburg. The information came from ladies from escort agencies that the group had brought to their hide outs. A special squad of police surrounded a house in Houghton early in the morning with snipers taking up strategic positions. They went into the house. McCall was the only occupant and he ran from window to window firing at the police. A desperate gun battle took place which the police ended by throwing stun grenades into the house. On entry, they found McCall dead on the floor. He had apparently shot himself because he was not going back to jail.

A day later the police found a second safe house and learnt of the plan to sell the yacht from a crew member who was to sail it to Fort Lauderdale. The boat was seized by police in Cape Town. Things had unravelled quickly for the gang after their photos appeared in the press, and Stander then made a further mistake. He had forged American documents and was passing himself off as an Australian writer when he bought a second hand Ford Mustang in Fort Lauderdale, but he drove the car without licensing it. He was stopped by the police and found to have a forged driver's licence. He was arrested but released after the car was impounded. Stander then displayed a total disregard for the police by breaking into the police car pound and driving off with his car.

The next day he went back to the second hand car dealer and asked him to respray the car another colour. The second hand car dealer had just seen an article in the local paper reporting that a famous bank robber from South Africa, Stander, was believed to be in Fort Lauderdale. When Stander walked in, the dealer suspected that the Australian was actually Stander. The Mustang was left with the dealer who phoned the police. That night a specialist squad of police surrounded Stander's apartment. Stander rode up to the apartment on a bicycle and was stopped by a policeman. Stander tried to disarm the policeman of his shotgun, but during the struggle Stander was shot and bled to death in the street. Things had gone rapidly wrong for Stander and his gang. It was barely two weeks from the time that the new photos from the robbery were circulated to when McCall and Stander were dead.

Alan Heyl left South Africa at the same time as Stander, going first to Greece and then on to England where he robbed a company of its payroll, but the amount was less than he expected. He decided to hide out in Spain, where he met up with other British underworld figures who offered to help him for a fee, before tipping off the police and Heyl was arrested outside London. Heyl served time in jail in England and was deported to South Africa where he served more time in jail before being released in 2005.

The Stander gang had operated like the American gangsters in the 1930s where a list of "public enemies" or "America's most wanted" criminals robbed banks, stole cars, and shot it out with local law enforcement and the FBI. Stander used his knowledge of police procedures to rob banks, and felt contempt for his fellow police officers, but he took too many chances, and in the end lost his fight for a policeman's firearm.

For the three years that Stander robbed banks in Durban, Dog Unit colleagues attended robberies at bank and building society branches; always a little too late. I wonder what would have happened if Vince Zimmerman did catch up with Stander in his getaway car after his first robbery, or if other dog cars had pulled him over in a random check after a robbery. I am sure that he would have tried to race away, and I am equally sure that the chase could have resulted in other cars being damaged and civilians hurt.

The irony is that a shoot-out could have occurred between a Police Dog Handler and the son of the man who commanded the Dog Units. Stander was like many hard core serious criminals. He was self-centred, cold and manipulative. He had a hedonistic life-style not caring how he got money. His double life of being a sole bank robber and keeping his secret from everyone for three years takes a special psychological make up. He had no concern for other people especially after escaping from jail, and his bloody end was the likely outcome of his recklessness. It was good fortune that so few people were injured during the gangs' rampage.

32
___

DUTY OFFICER IN THE FLYING SQUAD

During May 1977, I wrote and passed the 2 outstanding subjects for promotion to Lieutenant and was ordered to report to the Police College in Pretoria towards the end of June for the three month Officer Course. I travelled up to Pretoria in my Chev Kommando a few days ahead of the panel interview to see my former Commander Major Hennie Meyer who was in a senior staff role in the Dog School. Meyer had suggested that the Durban Dog Unit candidates all see him for an informal briefing to help us understand and prepare for the interview and the course. He gave us an outline of who was on the panel and what type of questions they could ask.

The course commenced with the interview in front of a selection board of two Generals and two Brigadiers. The Chairman of the panel was Senior Deputy Commissioner Geldenhuys, who became the Commissioner the following year. They had my personnel file in front of them which would have prompted the questions that they asked me. The discussions were almost entirely in Afrikaans, but I was comfortable in their presence and with the questions asked. My file was void of any allegations of misconduct or complaint, and I felt that my service in the Dog Unit would stand me in good stead.

I recall that one of the questions enquired about my drinking habits, and another about where I would like to be posted if I successfully completed the course. I told the Chairman that I would like to go back to the Dog Unit in Durban as a Duty Officer at Radio Control. My reasoning was that I had a vast amount of local knowledge and being English speaking was very important in Durban. The Chairman replied that they would consider this but said, "Jy kan nie jou hele loopbaan in 'n hond se poephol kyk nie!" This translated into English was that I could not spend my whole career looking up my dog's arse.

I was annoyed at the time as I enjoyed the job and loved my dog, and felt that I was really making a major difference to crime combating and prevention. Some years later I understood the wisdom of his words that we grow when we move on to other jobs and new challenges. I also later realised that to have taken another dog after Bruno retired would have locked me into a six or seven year commitment. I would not have wanted to develop an attachment, and then have to pass the dog on to another Handler if I saw the opportunity to move onto something else. I had a growing awareness that I was outgrowing my Dog Unit days, and it would be time to move on once Bruno was no longer fit to work.

I returned to Durban in October 1977 after passing the Officer Course with an Officer's commission signed by the State President, and two new shiny stars on each shoulder. I was assigned to Radio Station as Duty Officer. This was an important role because all policemen at stations and in vehicles had access to their Station Commanders during the day but would refer to the Duty Officer for guidance after normal office hours. My focus was on managing the Indoor Control Room staff, to provide advice and guidance on matters of law or procedure, and to attend to all police shooting incidents, and all police vehicle accidents. I would decide, depending on the seriousness of an incident, when District Commissioners or senior officers would be phoned in the middle of the night, or to call out specialist units. On night shifts and on weekends, I would drive around visiting various police stations checking on: staffing levels; complaints recorded in the Occurrence Book; prisoners in police cells and such like. I would also be listening to radio messages, together with complaints directed to police vehicles, and reports back.

Of the four duty officers at Radio Control, two were ordinary uniformed officers, whilst Manie Odendaal and I were Dog Handler officers. There were 2 vehicles for the officers; one car with fitted kennels, and a similar vehicle without kennels. We followed the same procedure of having two officers allocated to each vehicle to ensure equal mileage and maintenance.

One of the officers was disliked by his shift because he was very critical, lacked a team attitude and did not encourage or lead his indoor or flying squad staff. I only had dealings with him when we handed over to one another from time to time, so his personality was not an issue. Manie and I found that he took a liking to driving around with our dog car. We spoke to him about it, but he took no notice. We Dog Unit officers always ensured that our cars were spotlessly clean, but our colleague did not. I wondered how far we would have to go to make our point.

Late one afternoon before he came on duty for the night shift, I took Bruno out to heed the call of nature. He left a steaming deposit in the grass which I gathered onto a cardboard box and placed under the kennel in the car. I picked up my colleague with all the windows open and asked him to park my vehicle and take the other car. He picked me up the following morning with his assigned vehicle and complained that he had to use that vehicle because the dog car smelled bad. He got the unsubtle message

My shift Indoor Supervisor was a Warrant Officer who had been in the same position when I was a young Constable at Umbilo, and he had been on the bush course with me in 1970. He had a good team of young people with him made up of 3 or 4 Constables who had been out of college for a year or two, and 2 female clerical assistants. The Supervisor was known to have a drinking problem. He would have a secret stash in his car and would sneak out during his shift to have a swig from a bottle. He would never have too much to drink that his condition would cause a problem, and because he was very knowledgeable and got on well with his team, no one reported him.

I realised that his drinking may present me with a problem especially as the Duty Officer spent most of his time out on the road. The morning shift would be OK because the Officer Commanding Radio Control and admin personnel were present. Afternoon shifts would probably be OK, but the night shift would be a problem particularly if it became quiet after 1 or 2 am. I decided to take him in the car with me on night shifts. I told him that he needed to get out more and give some of the other indoor staff the opportunity of taking responsibility. I did this for several nights and returned to the office around 4 or 5 am to write up reports and returns. He would apparently go to his car after I left to pick up my replacement and gulp down vodka.

The Duty Officer came on duty an hour before the rest of his shift to provide cover over the shift handover. The 4 shift Duty Officers would pick one another up at our homes and drop the outgoing Officer off at his home. One evening I had been picked up for the night shift when the afternoon shift Indoor Supervisor came on the air and asked me to see him as soon as possible. He took me into a back room and there was my Indoor Supervisor. He had been dropped off at Radio Control by his son and was visibly worse for drink. The afternoon shift staff were looking to see what this new young Duty Officer would do. The Supervisor had a cut above his eye from a fall and I knew that I had no option but to default him and report his conduct.

I told him what I was going to do, and he tried to argue with me. I took his pocket book and made an appropriate entry in it. I drove him home and left a report for the Major who was the Commander of Radio Control. The Major now had the dilemma and arranged for him to be admitted to an alcohol dependant's institution. I had been tested but had done the right thing with compassion for the man, and with a sense of responsibility to the police organisation. The Supervisor was known to almost every policeman in Durban, as was his drinking problem, but it took a new Officer to take appropriate action.

My status as Duty Officer with a dog was creating some confusion for the Divisional Headquarters. I received a phone call from the Officer who nominated policemen for counter insurgency duties in South West Africa and other border areas where terrorists were exiting or entering the country. He wanted me to report to Pretoria for a four month tour. I asked if I was to go with or without the dog, as the Dog School in Pretoria would have to mobilise me with the dog or give permission for me to leave the dog back in Durban. That fell into the category of "too difficult", so some other Officer probably got the posting. I knew that I was an unusual case as I had attended a number of counter insurgency courses but had not yet been on a tour of duty in an operational area. I knew that I would have to go at some time.

My reputation as a capable Dog Handler prepared to enter any crime situation took on new dimension as a responsible Officer who would ensure that proper order and procedures were applied irrespective of past affiliations. It was a hard call to make however I had been placed in similar situations previously and I knew that I had to do the right thing for the good order of policing, my own reputation and the wellbeing of the Supervisor. The Supervisor's treatment was successful; he apparently never drank again and retired a few years later.

In early 1978 I bought a house in Fenniscowles Road, Umbilo. I had lived in the Umbilo and Glenwood area for the last six years of my schooling and after I joined the police. It was a solid working class area with roomy houses on quarter acre plots so there was a fair size garden to keep a dog.

I obtained permission to take Bruno out of kennels and keep him at home. The Dog Unit dropped off a kennel which I kept on the patio leading off the lounge. I received a bag of dry dog food every few weeks and occasionally bought large bones for him. He fitted into home life immediately. If someone walked into the yard with an air of confidence, Bruno would stand next to him as he rang the doorbell. If someone approached the gate and was hesitant, he would bark, and I would come out.

I had no fears about him biting anyone and he was really gentle with my baby son who would pull on him and hug him. Bruno knew the difference between on duty and off duty. We usually started a shift cycle with an afternoon shift. Bruno would see me with civvies clothes in the morning and when he saw me come out to the front verandah in uniform with my torch and other kit, he would run around the yard with joy knowing that the squad car was about to arrive and we were going to drive around.

With the comings and goings of the squad car, people in the area got to know that a policeman lived in the area and some would come to my house or chat when they saw me waiting to get picked up for duty. Some of them would raise complaints about neighbours or talk about items stolen and expect me to resolve their problems. I had to be sympathetic to a degree, but I was not the local police station to be called upon at all hours and I referred some of them to the local Charge Office or detectives.

There were some policing issues close to home that I could not ignore.

One night about midnight I was woken by shouting and the most blood curdling screams that sounded as though they were coming from a house backing onto my yard. I jumped out of bed, barefoot and only in a pair of shorts, grabbed a torch and ran out the front gate where Bruno was standing waiting. I recognised the cries of an African woman that sounded like someone was administering a beating to her. We ran down Fenniscowles Road into Fleming Johnstone Road following the sound of the cries.

I saw an African woman who had run onto the front verandah of a house that abutted the side of my property. She was cowering and was being thrashed by an African man. I ran onto the verandah and stepped between the woman and the man, who backed into a corner in fear of the dog. I commanded Bruno to sit and he sat there like a sprinter in the starting blocks waiting to be released. The man dropped a sjambok which he was using to beat the woman. A sjambok is a leather whip originally made from hippo or other animal hide and used to drive cattle. This sjambok was a shorter version made of plastic but could still inflict a very painful beating.

I saw my neighbours peeping through the window as I searched the man for any concealed weapons. I felt completely safe in this situation for although Bruno was sitting at my command, he would fly into the man if he was stupid enough to attempt to strike or attack me. I used a mixture of Zulu and English to ask the woman and the man what the problem was. It appeared that the man and woman were lovers and he had reason to believe that she was seeing someone else. That was too much for Zulu male pride to bear so he kept the house where she worked as a domestic under observation and followed her to another house in the area.

He had then confronted her, and she ran off down the street towards her place of employment with her lover in pursuit laying into her with the sjambok. I asked the neighbours to phone the police and the patrol van from Umbilo took them off to the station for her to lay a charge and for the man to be detained. I felt that notwithstanding the beating, the woman would probably open a case but withdraw it a few days later.

———

On another occasion, I woke up when I heard Bruno make a whimpering sound at the front gate. I looked out the bedroom window and saw Bruno looking down the street. I could pinpoint what was happening by looking between his ears and using his snout like a gun sight. He was letting me know that someone was creeping around the cars across the road. He looked back at the window and saw me peeping at him through a crack in the curtain and he knew that I would come out. I saw that it was around one in the morning as I quickly pulled on a t-shirt and a pair of running shoes. I went into the garden via the lounge patio door and stood next to Bruno and looked in the direction that he was indicating to me. I could not see anyone in the street and there were no cars moving about. I remained in the shadows at the gate, staring in the direction of a number of cars parked about 60 or 70 metres down the street.

I could not see anything, but Bruno knew that someone was there. I suspected that there were car breakers at work. We quietly went into the street and immediately crossed over to the far side to use the row of parked cars as cover as we moved to the area that Bruno had indicated. As we got to about 20 meters from the spot, a young White male ran off at high speed. I called out to him to stop or I would release the dog. He ran into a yard and then jumped a number of fences into other properties. I did not release Bruno as I was not suitably dressed to start jumping fences. I decided to check the cars in the immediate vicinity for tampering and then to call other Dog Unit vehicles to surround and search the area if required.

I found a 10 litre petrol container with a siphon pipe in the petrol tank of a parked car. A damaged petrol cap lay in the gutter next to the container. I saw at least two other vehicles with petrol caps removed and realized that the culprit had probably more than one container and would have his car parked somewhere in the area. Because there were two other cars with removed petrol caps and signs of petrol spillage, I expected that he had already taken a full container to his own vehicle. I walked back up the street looking at parked cars checking for warm exhaust pipes to indicate the thief's car. I got to a car with a warm exhaust about 100 meters away from the crime scene and saw a young woman apparently asleep in the front seat.

Bingo! Years of experience and knowledge of criminal habits develops one's intuition and I was not let down. I knocked on the window, identified myself as policeman and asked her why she was sitting in the car. She proceeded to tell me a story about her boyfriend visiting someone in the nearby block of flats. I asked her which flat and who the occupant was and proceeded to demolish her quickly thought out cover story. I saw that she had a long dress which was arranged to conceal something under her legs. I asked her to get out of the car and found there was another container full of petrol. I asked where the petrol came from and she continued to produce a flow of silly explanations. I looked at her in a quizzical manner and shook my head, and she knew that the game was up.

I asked her about her boyfriend, and she told me that they had no money and needed to get back to Johannesburg. I knew that the boyfriend would return to where he parked the car to see if the police arrived or if I had left the area, so I told her to get back in the car and stay there. Bruno and I stood back into the shadows near the flats entrance foyer and waited in the dark. About 10 minutes later, I saw the man returning from the direction in which he had run. He was trying to creep up to his car using the parked cars as cover. He could not see any movement or activity in the vicinity, so he thought that he had got away with it. I waited until he got to the car and opened the door and when the girlfriend pointed in our direction, I stepped out into the streetlights. There was no fight or flight left in him and he gave up with a deep sigh.

I waved across to my house and indicated to my wife to phone the police. A few minutes later a police dog car raced up Fennis-cowles Road and stopped. Residents in the area had been alerted by the sound of the suspect running off with me in pursuit and had now come out into the street when the squad car stopped. Neighbours identified their cars and gave their particulars to my colleague who then took the couple to the police station.

———

The level of unrest and rioting in townships had subsided some months after the Soweto riots in June 1976, but activists and the ANC encouraged civil disobedience in the run up to the anniversary in June 1977. A number of activists and black community leaders were arrested throughout the country. One such activist was Steve Biko. Stephen Biko was a noted anti-apartheid activist. He was born in King Williams Town, in the Eastern Cape and was a student at the University of Natal Medical School. He was initially involved with the multiracial National Union of South

African Students, but after he became convinced that Black, Indian and Coloured students needed an organization of their own, he helped found the South African Students' Organization (SASO) in 1968.

SASO evolved into the influential Black Consciousness Movement (BCM). Biko was banned during March 1973, meaning that he was not allowed to speak to more than one person at a time, was restricted to certain areas, and could not make speeches in public. It was also forbidden to quote anything he said, including speeches or simple conversations.

In the aftermath of the Soweto riots, security police began to target Biko further. On 18 August 1977, he was arrested at a police roadblock in the Eastern Cape under the Terrorism Act. He suffered a major head injury while in police custody and was chained to a window grille for a full day. On 11 September 1977 police loaded him into the back of a car and began the long drive to Pretoria. He died shortly after the arrival in the Pretoria prison. Police claimed his death was the result of an extended hunger strike. He was found to have massive injuries to the head which many saw as strong evidence that he had been heavily and brutally clubbed.

Due to his fame, news of his death quickly spread across the world. His funeral was attended by many hundreds of people, including numerous ambassadors and other diplomats from the United States and Western Europe. Journalist Donald Woods, a personal friend of Biko, photographed his injuries in the morgue and was later forced to flee South Africa for England, where he campaigned against apartheid and further publicized Biko's life and death

I went to visit my dad when I returned from the Officer Course in Pretoria in the October and he asked me about the Biko case and what the police had done to cause his death. I had no information other than what was in the newspapers, but I found myself looking for excuses for the policemen involved but I knew that I could not defend the indefensible. Dad quietly said that whatever way you looked at the case, the police had a lot to answer for. I knew that he was right. He then said, "My boy, you cannot remain in an organisation that does this sort of thing." I knew that he was right again, but I was not one of those policemen. I had just been made an Officer and had a wife and child; how could I leave now when policing was all that I knew since leaving school?

There were lots of policemen of all races, who like me only wanted to be good policemen and to serve our communities. Was this an excuse for lack of confidence in my ability to adapt to possible work opportunities in commerce, or was I only trying to get along with my life? I initially only joined the police to fulfil my National Service commitment but enjoyed what I was doing, was good at it, and was progressing up the ranks. I realised that whilst I had no answers at that immediate time, I would have to consider other employment options in the future as they presented themselves; but I would have to learn new skills and gain broader experience to be ready to take the right opportunity.

33

SEARCH FOR THE BEACH RAPIST

Z inkwazi is a beach side village some 70 kilometres North of Durban which is an ideal holiday venue for those who want quiet secluded beaches away from the hustle and bustle of the city. The North Coast highway has a turnoff with a road that runs for seven kilometres through farmland and natural bush to the village of less than a hundred houses and a handful of small hotels beside the river estuary with long sandy beaches; an ideal off the beaten track holiday venue.

On a Sunday afternoon in January 1978 a 16 year old holiday maker from Rhodesia (Zimbabwe) decided to walk along the beach. No one in her family wanted to accompany her and as it was a hot sunny day, she decided to go off on her own wearing her bikini. The beach was deserted, and she was enjoying the quiet solitude of sun, sea and nature.

Suddenly, a young man holding a knife ran out from the bush on the dunes and grabbed her dragging her into the surf. She struggled with him, but he was too strong for her and he then held her under the water. She felt that she was drowning and became weak at which point he dragged her out of the surf and up into the bushes. He grabbed her by the throat and throttled her before stabbing her in the left breast, and then proceeded to rape her. When he got off her she took her chances and ran off back in the direction of the village. The rapist did not follow her.

Her family contacted the local Police station in Stanger and related what happened. The police at Stanger realised that the environment and secluded nature of the area would be best searched by a dog and contacted the Police Radio Control in Durban.

The Durban Dog Unit did not routinely patrol or respond to complaints that far North of the city. The Dog Unit assigned patrol areas to their members and rotated the areas to members of the shift. A typical dog unit shift would assign 4 or 5 vehicles to Durban Central, with a dog vehicle to North Durban, South Durban, Inner West and Outer West areas to respond to serious crime or cases where a dog's enhanced senses would more likely provide a successful outcome.

Constable Doug Linden, a nine year police veteran and his dog Ceazer were covering the North Durban area and were despatched to attend. Linden and his dog had been a team for nearly 4 years and had the experience to follow up on this case. The Stanger Police were asked to secure the area near where the rape took place to keep a possible scent intact for the arrival of the dog.

At that time, the squad cars mostly in use were Valiant Chrysler sedans with a Charger engine fitted with twin Weber carburettors or a six cylinder 4.1 litre Chevrolet. The squad car could reach speeds in excess of 200 kilometres per hour and with an open road, Linden and Ceazer were on the scene in less than 30 minutes. The Stanger Police identified the crime scene to Linden who put Ceazer on a puppy line, a light leash of about 10 metres in length used for tracking. Ceazer quickly picked up a scent which lead them through the natural bush which was a tangle of trees, roots and thickets of bush with visibility restricted to only a few metres.

Following the scent in that environment was ideal as it was unlikely that anyone else would be in the area to confuse the dog and it would be unlikely that anyone would be in that area with a plausible reason. Years of working with a dog develops a unique partnership where Handler and dog read one another. As Ceazer started to increase his pace Linden knew it meant that the scent was fresh, and they were getting closer to their quarry. After about a kilometre from the point where they had entered the bush Ceazer caught a glimpse of a man trying to hide in a tree and barked indicating he had found the suspect. The man who was naked, heard the dog bark so jumped down and ran off. Ceazer was released off the puppy line and went in for the tackle grabbing the man by his leg and dropping him. The man kicked free and ran on with the dog in pursuit. Ceazer tackled him again. The naked man struggled to get loose and tried to continue his escape, but Linden had caught up and dived onto the man. The desperate man punched Linden in the face and a rough and tumble ensued with punches, kicks and bites going in. Linden overpowered the man and handcuffed him.

Constable Doug Linden with Ceazer

It is unusual for a dog to be set on a naked person. When a dog goes in for a tackle, they look to grab an arm or a leg, and a person's clothing gives the dog something to hang onto until the Handler can grab a suspect and arrest him. It was therefore not surprising that a dog may have difficulty in tackling a naked person particularly when they are unconcerned about injuries and desperate to get away.

Linden took his subdued prisoner back to the beach and the scene of the crime. They began a search for the knife and the man's clothing. Searching for objects in sand dunes covered with foliage can be a difficult task but that situation is also one of the skills taught to a patrol dog. The Handler will direct the dog by using hand signals, pointing in various directions and the dog will use his sense of smell to search for a foreign object. The dog hones in on the scent of the suspect that he has helped to arrest.

In a short time Ceazer indicated an area where the man had buried his knife and clothing which were recovered as evidence. In this case, the patrol dog had demonstrated most of its trained capability. Using police dog terminology he had successfully tracked a suspect, had "barked out" and identified the suspect and tackled him when he fled. Then the dog was then used in a "squaring exercise" to search out and identify hidden items of evidence.

The complainant identified her attacker and the knife. The young lady received medical assistance for her wound and the family shortly thereafter returned home. She declined to return to South Africa to give evidence in the subsequent court case but with the testimony of the policemen, the evidence of the clothing, the knife and the medical reports, her attacker was convicted and sentenced to 2 years in prison. The policemen who attended the scene felt that if the man had not been caught then, it was highly probable that he would have continued to stalk lone women on the beach and that saved others from a similar fate.

34

BRUNO STABBED AGAIN

I realised that my role as Duty Officer at Radio Control would require me to lead and guide rather than being first at the crime scene. Bruno was still very fit but was getting on in dog years. We were good company for each other when on duty and he was my protection as the Duty Officer usually travelled alone. I was working a night shift at the end of May 1978 and was about to head back to the office to write up my visits and inspections at around 4am when a controller asked for a dog vehicle to attend a report of a car breaking in progress, in the vicinity of Hillary which was a suburb to the South West of Durban. Most vehicles were some distance away or standing off at stations following up other complaints. I told control that I would attend and that another vehicle should be despatched to the scene as back up.

The controller kept the complainant on the telephone and was giving me updated information as the man moved from vehicle to vehicle along Smerden Place. As I approached the area I reduced speed and turned off my car lights. I stopped about a block away and approached the area where the man was last seen. I had Bruno on his leash and carried my torch as the sky was turning a slight red colour just before dawn. I could see a trail of 3 or 4 cars that had smashed windows. Pieces of glass sparkled on the ground like diamonds in the street lighting as I approached a vehicle with the door slightly ajar. I looked into the car and saw a man in the front seat tugging on a radio fitted into the dashboard. I took out my pistol and tapped it on the window. The man looked at me with a surprised wide eyed look and immediately opened the door on the other side of the car.

I ran around and grabbed him by his jacket. He shook his jacket off and took off like a rabbit. I released Bruno who went after him in pursuit. I saw Bruno run in to take him by an arm and then saw the man smack at the dog. Bruno dropped back which was unusual for him. If a person tried to hit out at him with a stick or object, he would move across to the other side and take his other arm, or he would take him from the rear by his calf or thigh. I called out to Bruno to go in as I ran along the road at full speed.

There was a fence at the end of the road which the man and Bruno cleared, and the ground then dropped away down a steep 15 metre embankment. We had run onto the worksite of the Outer Ring Road freeway which was then under construction. The man ran and tumbled down the bank and I followed about 40 or 50 meters behind. I could see Bruno in the moonlight and early dawn light run in to tackle the man and again he backed off when struck. I then realised that the man was carrying a screwdriver and had struck Bruno at least twice. I tried to speed up as I reached the flat gravel of the road surface and was gaining on him.

Bruno continued to run in at him and then I suddenly felt something hit me in the legs like a rugby tackle from the front. I hit the ground with a heavy thud and tried immediately to get to my feet. I could feel blood running down one leg which was held firmly by a metal reinforcing rod. I thought that I had impaled my leg and was stuck on a metal stake. I tried to pull free and realised that the rod was not stuck in my leg but had tangled and tied up in my trousers. I tore my trouser leg loose and ran after the thief and Bruno.

Bruno had taken the man by his leg and they had fallen into a large open concrete lined storm water culvert on the side of the road. I jumped in to grab the man and help Bruno. I punched out at the man and hit him high on his forehead almost breaking my right hand. I grabbed his right arm expecting that he still held the screwdriver. Whilst struggling with the man, I felt Bruno brushing against me as we both attempted to overpower him. Bruno's fur was wet and sticky with blood, but he had hold of the man by a leg and was biting into him. The man was fighting desperately to get away and it was a case of Bruno and I taking control of him, or him getting away after leaving us stabbed and injured, possibly seriously, in a ditch in the dark.

Bruno stabbed in the neck and thigh

I swung a punch into his stomach with my left fist because my right was damaged. I felt it sink in and wind him, but he was fighting like a crazy man. He was kicking and trying to punch at me as I held his arms. I wanted to ensure that he no longer had the screwdriver in his hands and that he could not reach into a pocket to remove a knife or gun. I punched again with a clubbing left to the head. The impact caused my watch to fly off. I had him against the side of the culvert and grabbed him by his ears and banged his head against the concrete. I heard other Dog Handlers calling out as they ran towards me and then became conscious of another dog next to me grabbing on to the man. At that stage the man realised that the fight was up and Constable Frans Gunther jumped down into the drain, pinned his arms behind him and handcuffed him.

I felt very weak and shaky from the adrenalin of the fight and the injury. I did not know the extent of my injury at that time but was most concerned for Bruno. I helped him out of the culvert and with the aid of a torch saw a bloody patch on a hind leg and another in the neck. I parted the fur and saw the puncture wounds. I checked my leg and examined a gash on my leg which whilst still bleeding was not too deep. Control contacted our vet and he was waiting for me at the clinic to operate on Bruno immediately. Both wounds were very deep, with the one on his hind leg affecting the muscle that would need time to heal. I went to the hospital and received an anti-tetanus injection, had my wound dressed and fortunately did not require any stitches.

The accused, Anthony Vezi, appeared in court several weeks later and pleaded guilty to two counts of attempted theft and two counts of theft involving stealing cassette player/radios from motor cars. He pleaded not guilty to a charge of malicious injury to property relating to the stabbing of Bruno resulting in veterinary costs of R69.45. Bruno was considered to be Government property hence the nature of the charge. The Magistrate took all four counts of theft and attempted theft as one for the purpose of sentence, as well as previous convictions and jailed him for four years. He received a further fine of R200 or nine months imprisonment for stabbing Bruno.

Bruno was left at home to convalesce for two to three weeks as I was only away from work for a week. The Dog Unit men did not take much sick leave in those days. We couldn't wait to get back to work; even if it meant limping around for a few days. Friends came to the house to visit and look at Bruno's stitches in his wounds which were very visible with the hair shaved off. My son was less than 2 years old at the time, but he heard me talking about Bruno being stabbed with a screwdriver and knew what a screwdriver was. I was horrified one day to see him with a screwdriver in his hand prodding Bruno in the leg near his wound. One would expect the dog to savage the child, but he only made a whimpering noise and got up and walked off.

35

A DANGEROUS WOMAN

A murder case made the headlines in 1978 where a young woman was charged with the murder of her father. Police found that a young woman had shot and killed her father with a nine millimetre pistol. It appeared to be an open and shut case of murder notwithstanding that the young woman, Louise Carol Butler-Smith, claimed self-defence alleging that her father sexually molested her.

Butler-Smith's defence provided a sordid narrative of how her father had raped her and she was driven to the extreme and shot him. The sensational case was widely reported in the media and was a topic of much discussion. In the absence of contrary evidence and a convincing display in court, she was found not guilty and discharged. Her firearm and ammunition was returned to her.

Several months later in 1979 police received a report of a shooting at Anna Capri flats in St Andrews Street near Albert Park. A flat on the third floor was occupied by a young couple, and when the boyfriend arrived home he found the front door locked from the inside. He inserted his key and tried to unlock the door and was greeted by a volley of shots fired through the front door, with one of the bullets hitting him in the arm wounding him severely. He fled the flats running across the road to a restaurant looking for help. The proprietor phoned the police and the ambulance service, and related what the young man had told him.

The report was received by Sergeant Vince Zimmerman, Constable Doug Linden and Sergeant Nicky Kleynhans of the Durban Dog Unit. On their arrival they were told by the boyfriend that he believed his girlfriend, Louise Carol Butler-Smith, had shot him intentionally. The boyfriend was taken to hospital and the policemen went up to the flat and approached the front door carefully ready to respond to any situation that may be thrown at them. They noticed that the door had a number of bullet holes with exit splinters on the outside at mid height around the area of the door handle and lock.

The policemen took cover behind the brick wall near the front door and knocked on the door with a baton to minimise the possibility of being injured if the knocking response was more shots fired through the door. There was no reply, so they called out identifying themselves as policemen and calling for the occupant to respond and open the door. The top part of the door had clear glass with a lace curtain on the inside giving a measure of privacy, but the policemen realised that anyone inside the flat would see them at the door. After further knocking and calling met with no response, Kleynhans left to collect tear gas whilst Zimmerman and Linden held their position.

Zimmerman decided to smash the window near the lock to see what response that elicited and as a possible way to put a hand inside to unlock the latch, if the situation presented itself. They were still uncertain if the woman was waiting for them to expose themselves so she could shoot at them, if she was conscious or alive or whether some other person was in the flat waiting to shoot whoever exposed themselves. The policemen stood behind the cover of the wall with their pistols drawn in case they need to return fire to protect themselves.

Zimmerman resorted to an old cowboy trick of putting his cap on his baton and raising it to the window to see if it attracted any fire. He did this a few times and when nothing happened he exposed his hand by putting it through the window and released the lock to open the door. They continued to call out to any occupant that they were armed and coming into the flat. Zimmerman entered the flat with Linden closely behind him providing cover. They found a woman in the flat who was identified as Louise Butler-Smith, took her into custody and recovered her pistol and ammunition. The weapon was the same pistol that she used to kill her father.

Linden and Zimmerman take cover whilst trying to get access to the flat. Note the keys in the door and the bullet holes near the door handle.

Unbeknown to the policemen, a newspaper photographer, Terry Hayward of the Natal Mercury, had picked up information of the incident and went to the scene. He went to a nearby block of flats and found a good vantage point overlooking the flat door where Zimmerman and Linden were huddled. Using his telephoto lens, he took a number of photos including the one above. That photo together with a photo of Zimmerman with his cap off made front page news the following morning. The Durban public were very positive about the capability of the Dog Unit and the Flying Squad. This report with action photos enhanced that reputation giving the public a real sense of confidence and trust in their police.

But with all good cases, you cannot please them all.

Zimmerman was queried by an Officer as to why he removed his cap during the operation implying that he was improperly dressed.

Butler-Smith was charged with attempted murder and some months later appeared in court to answer the charge. Her defence was patently false, and she changed her story a number of times. When she saw that her version was improbable and things were not going her way, she shouted at the judge and left the court room by descending down into the prisoner cell area and refused to attend the proceedings any further. She was convicted and sentenced to five years imprisonment. This case and her behaviour raised the belief that she was a liar and that her portrayal of her father may have been untrue resulting in her getting away with murder.

Sergeant Vince Zimmerman leads Butler-Smith from the flat.

36

LOVERS' LANE ROBBERS SURPRISE

T he Golden Mile ran along the Marine Parade between the
beach and rows of hotels. This was the tourist magnet that
made Durban the preferred holiday destination for South
Africans living inland around Johannesburg, Pretoria and the
Orange Free State. The holiday makers were important to the
economy and reputation of Durban. The upmarket hotels were on
the northern end of the Marine Parade and the more economic
hotels were around the southern end near the large Addington
hospital. There was an area of undeveloped sports fields at the
southern end near the run down Point area which was used as a
spill over car park on busy days at the beaches.

This space was unlit and was sometimes used as a lovers' lane
area for couples to make out in their cars. It was generally safe and
was often used as a park off area by Dog Handlers patrolling the
beachfront area late at night so the dogs could relieve themselves
on the 10 hour night shift.

Late one evening in January 1979, Radio Control despatched a
member of C shift Dog Unit to attend a report of a robbery at the
Addington sports fields. On arrival they met a young couple who
had been cuddling in a car on the dark sports field when a

window was smashed, and the door jerked open. They were confronted by at least two men armed with knives who took their money, watches and jewellery. The couple were taken to the local Point Police Station and a case of robbery was registered. Other members of C shift patrolled the area but could not find any likely suspects as there were very few people in the area.

A few nights later a further report of a robbery at the sports field was passed on to a member of C shift. Another couple had been robbed in the same manner and had suffered injuries before handing over their money. The shift got together sometime later to discuss the case. The fear that the victims suffered made an impact on the usually unemotional policemen. There was also a sense that the criminals had got away with the robbery and the Dog Handlers had not been able to find them. This was a challenge to their crime combatting ability, with a realisation that the criminals were going to continue to rob lovers believing that uniform patrols were not going to catch them.

The shift collectively decided that as their rest days were coming up they would set a trap using a bait car with lovers, and as the area was open and away from buildings, dogs would be hidden at various points some distance away. Sergeants Vince Zimmerman and Pieter Du Plooy together with Constables Paddy O'Brien, Len Hutton and Kevin Whittock and their dogs would be the response group whilst Constables Doug Linden and Mark Wood would be the lovers. There was much debate and joking in the group about who would play the role of the woman and eventually Linden gave in. Linden wore a long red wig, a dress with a stuffed bra and high heel shoes to look the part but he refused to wear make-up.

He later told a newspaper reporter that make-up would not be required in the dark but it may have clashed with his moustache. He said, "I didn't mind the woman's disguise because we knew that it would bring results. We were sick and tired of seeing people beaten up and robbed by thugs at the sports field". That summed up the feelings of the group and the determination not to let this criminal gang get away. They also realised that criminals were acting with impunity and would be stupid enough to continue in the belief that they would not get caught.

This was the challenge that C shift was going to take up. The team decided to deploy to the sports field around 9pm. As agreed, Linden and Wood drove onto the sports field in Wood's car whilst the other members parked their private cars with their dogs at different spots around the sports fields. If the robbers ran off in any direction, they would run into one of the policemen and their dogs. The team had portable radios to keep in touch, to report any suspicious movement and to call in the response team when the robbers struck.

Members of "C" shift who staged the Lovers Lane surprise. Front row: Doug Linden and Mark Wood (The Lovers). Back Row: Constable Paddy O'Brien, Sergeant Pieter Du Plooy, Sergeant Vince Zimmerman, Constables Len Hutton and Kevin Whittock (The Back-up).

Linden and Wood parked the car on the dark field and proceeded to "make out" whilst looking around to see if they could spot any movement in the dark. Radios were on and everyone settled down to wait. After an hour with nothing happening, Linden and Wood decided to get out the car and walk around holding hands and then spread a blanket on the ground and lay down for the benefit of any watchers. After a while they got back into the car realising that being in the car they would have some protection and some time to respond if the robbers tried to get the doors open.

Stake outs can be a mixture of boredom whilst waiting and tension that something may happen requiring a quick response.

There is also a feeling that you cannot be over confident as something could go wrong and the "lovers" were placing themselves at risk of injury.

Around 11pm, Linden and Wood saw two men approach the car. One of the robbers smashed a brick on the side window whilst the other jerked open the door on Linden's side of the car, brandishing a knife in his hand and demanding money. Linden's first response was to grab the man, but he stabbed Linden five times on the leg in quick succession. Linden was lucky that the robber was off balance and the stab wounds were not deep. The commotion and the action at the car was spotted by the response group who ran onto the field with their dogs. The robbers saw that they had fallen into a trap and ran off in separate directions, but the trap was well planned. Constable Paddy O'Brien released Rex who brought one of the men down, whilst Constable Len Hutton released Wagter who brought down the other. Both men were taken into custody and taken to the Point Police station.

Linden received medical attention at the nearby Addington hospital and with his dress in a mess, joined his colleagues at the police station. There was much joking and laughing at Linden in his drag outfit by his colleagues and other policemen at the station as a mixture of released adrenalin and satisfaction in a job well done.

The cohesion and success of the men of C shift and their dedication in giving up their day off was reported in the local press and did much to add to the confidence that the public felt in their police service.

37

MATTERS OF LIFE AND DEATH

The Dog Unit's priority complaints were attending burglar alarms, usually housebreaking at residential and business properties, and racing to crimes in progress; including robberies, car break ins or stolen cars. We also accompanied detectives to effect arrests, and tracked suspects in bush or semi rural areas. Dog Handlers were much more experienced and senior than the police station van drivers and were therefore usually despatched to more serious or complicated complaints. One such area was attending to reports of dead people.

A report of a dead person could have a range of reasons and outcomes including murder, natural causes or suicide, and required an experienced policeman as the first responder. The place where the body was found was a potential crime scene and likely items of evidence had to be preserved.

I was fresh out of Dog School when on a busy Saturday morning, I was despatched to a report that a woman had jumped off a building in West Street in Durban's main shopping area. I saw a fire engine and an ambulance parked near an arcade, so I parked the squad car behind them. A fireman directed me down the arcade towards a fire escape where I saw a team of firemen standing about two stories up the metal escape. I climbed up to them and saw the body of a young woman who appeared to have fallen from the roof about five floors above. I asked one of the firemen to accompany me up to the roof. The building had a flat roof with a parapet about three foot high around the edge. Just inside the parapet, close to the fire escape, we found a pair of shoes neatly placed together. I had learnt in conversations with older colleagues about a strange phenomena associated with women who jumped off buildings. They nearly always take their shoes off to climb over the parapet onto an outside ledge before they jump. It is as if they do not want to accidently fall when climbing over. They seem to want to get themselves steady on the ledge before making a conscious decision to jump.

I recovered the shoes and went down to the ledge where the woman's body was lying, when a detective from Durban Central Police Station arrived. I handed the shoes over to him and briefed him on what we found. He would take the case and investigate the circumstances to see if there was foul play, and to determine any likely reasons for her to take her own life. The firemen wrapped the body in blankets and lowered the woman to the ground to be taken away by the ambulance.

I was still living at home with my parents at the time and mentioned to them in passing that I had attended a likely suicide in town. A few days later my father told me that he had a phone call with a long standing friend whose daughter, whom I had met many years earlier, had committed suicide by jumping off a building in town. She had been suffering from post natal depression, and family and doctor support had not helped. A tragic and unnecessary loss. I wondered if I would have felt any differently if I had realised when I was on the fire escape who the young woman was.

———

Another difficult experience and sharp learning curve I recall fairly early in my police career was when I was required to go to an address at around two in the morning to tell the residents that their mother had died in the Addington Hospital, and ask them to contact the Ward Sister. I was asked to go and convey this message because the residents in the flat did not have a telephone. I felt ill at ease about this as I did not know if the news was expected or not. How do you knock on someone's door who you have never met and say, " Sorry but your mom is dead. Please contact the hospital"? As I drove there I thought about how I should start the conversation after they had opened the door.

I stopped at the address and walked up to the flat. I had an opening line sort of worked out but did not know if I just should ask them to contact the hospital, or to say that their mom had died. I braced myself and knocked. A woman came to the door. I said, "I have a message from the hospital", and before I could proceed any further the woman said, "Oh! Has my mom died?" I replied that she had and the woman thanked me as it appeared that they were expecting her to pass on at any time, and they were emotionally ready for that.

I walked back to the car feeling rather relieved, but I had learnt another lesson. If you have bad news, do not avoid the reality of the message but be ready for different responses. Be empathetic and offer what assistance you can. Ask if there is anyone you can contact, but there is no script that fits every situation.

———

I attended numerous cases involving death, and developed a professional detachment from events in order to be focussed, and not get distracted from getting the job done. Some cases however did occasionaly break through the emotional firewall.

Early one morning around 3 am, I received a call from Radio Control to go to an address in Puntans Hill where a member of the public reported that they found their neighbour dead in his car. I spoke with the complainant who told me that the neighbour was about eighty years of age, and had lost his wife about six months earlier after a long illness. The neighbours were on good terms with one another and they spoke regularly, but they reported that the man had lost interst in everything since his wife's death. They said that they had woken up hearing a car engine running in the neighbour's garage. The husband had gone next door into the garage and found the old man in the driver's seat, with a hosepipe running from the exhaust into the small fanlight window. All other windows in the car were closed. He had gassed himself.

The neighbour had switched off the engine, then opened the doors and windows to ventlate the car and garage. I found that the back door to the house was unlocked so I went in. The house was neat and tidy with photos of the couple at various stages in their long marriage. I noticed a number of sheets of writing paper on the dining room table. On examination, I saw that they contained his suicide note. He had written about twenty such notes with minor changes to words and sentence format, as though he wanted to be absolutely correct, and I thought, was in some way convincing himself to take his life. The notes had the singular theme, "I do not want to live without her".

The old gentleman was structured to the end by also providing names, addresses and telephone numbers of people to be contacted once he was found. I really felt for him and how he must have felt without his life partner, but returned to the task in hand. I waited for the ambulance to take him to hospital, then gathered up the notes, locked the house and garage, and gave the house and car keys to the neighbour to hold until the old gentleman's nominated next of kin arrived. I took the documents to the police station, wrote a statement for the detectives and handed the notes in. The detectives would need that information to prepare a case docket for an inquest.

———

Dealing with the dead is one thing but dealing with the dying is raw and pushes the emotional wall almost beyond its limit.

On a sunny and unremarkable day, I was patrolling in the area between New Germany and the Clermont Township. I approached an intersection and saw cars stopping, with drivers getting out to look down an embankment. I pulled over to the verge to find out what everyone was looking at. I looked down the embankment and saw a car on its roof with the wheels still spinning. I had just missed an accident, with one vehicle with a dented front stationary in the intersection, and another down the bank. I scrambled down to where the car had come to rest about five metres below the road level. As I approached the car I saw an African man lying just outside the car. He must have been the driver and had been thrown out of the car as it rolled down the bank.

Seat belts were only fitted in new cars in South Africa around 1970, and it was not a legal requirement for drivers and passengers to wear belts if older models were not fitted with seat belts. I went to the man who did not have any signs of blood but I could see that he was lying awkwardly. He seemed to be unconscious but as I got to him, he looked up at me with wide eyes and he grabbed my hands. I looked at him and said, "I've got you. Its OK". His face relaxed and he got the glimmer of a smile. I told him that an ambulance was on its way. I held his hand as he tried to say something then I felt his grip tighten and then loosen. He looked at me and I saw his eyes glaze over and he went limp. I said, "I've got you. God bless".

An ambulance arrived shortly thereafter and I helped put the man on a stretcher and carry him up the bank and he was taken off to hospital. It seemed so ironic when I drove off thinking that the international view was of White policemen and Black people in South Africa either hating or fearing one another. Yet here was a situation where our race or background did not count for anything. A man was critically hurt and he wanted someone to hold him and reassure him. We met as fellow human beings at a time of crisis, and I believe that I gave him a measure of care and comfort as he passed from this life. I had let my humanity and care out of the bag for a moment because the situation demanded it and because I felt it.

· · ·

I spent thirty years of my life learning about life and death, learning about the human condition and about what people do to one another. I kept this emotional barrier up to do the job, as did my colleagues. Day to day events touched us in one way or another. Some resulted in positive and uplifting feelings, whilst other tragic events dragged us down. I like to think that on occasions we made a bad day better for the people we came into contact with. The accumulation of the tough experiences and negative feelings were kept in a bag locked away in our subconscious. It probably created a numbing effect where we could empathise with people without feeling too much raw emotion. At times though, these feelings leaked out and I saw colleagues taking strain.

Post Traumatic Stress Disorder (PTSD) was unknown to us at that time. The closest was probably referred to as "combat fatigue". It was some years after the Vietnam war that psychologists and specialists identified PTSD and developed ways of treating sufferers.

The South African Police rotated a number of policemen on counter insurgency patrols in the Caprivi Strip in Namibia (South West Africa) near the confluence of the borders of Rhodesia, Angola, Zambia and Botswana which was a crossing point for African National Congress (ANC) and South West African Peoples Organisation (SWAPO) guerillas. A further group of South African policemen were deployed on counter insurgency patrols in Rhodesia in support of their forces from around 1968 to early 1975. Some of our colleagues came back from those four month tours of duty with a little edginess, and would overreact to loud unexpected noises.

Symptoms of stress on returning from border duties became known as "bos befok" literally meaning screwed up by the bush and abbreviated to "bossies". The police division of Port Natal had a Chaplain and a single Social Worker at that time who would deal with work and domestic related problems reported by commanding officers and affected policemen. At that time, the emphasis was on alcohol related problems which usually resulted in men being sent to an alcohol rehabilitation centre for a time.

The Dog Handlers were often exposed to horrific crime scenes with terrible injuries and mutilated bodies in vehicle accidents or house fires that left them a bit wobbly. Dealing with next of kin in a sympathetic manner and seeing their anguish added to our stress as we tried to be compassionate but professional, whilst keeping our own feelings in check. We had no protocols for dealing with these tough emotions other than our concern for one another and comeraderie as a group. We would band together on a rest day and go into the bush for a braai (BBQ) with several beers. We'd tell stories, laugh and be melancholy together and help one another through the darkness.

As the Dog Unit had more experienced members than the uniformed policemen at stations, we saw a lot more and as the first responders to serious crime we were on a state of alert every time we attended a crime in progress. Even the elite get worn down by constant exposure to crime scenes, danger and dealing with victims. I saw some colleagues develop drinking problems and domestic issues that negatively affected their lives and dragged them down.

The role of a policeman's wife or partner could also be difficult and their ability to read their husband's mood on returning from work was important. Family support and understanding was important for the well being of all policemen faced with bad days at the office. We need to salute the partners, and recognise their role in keeping us at the sharp end together and focussed as rational and fully functioning human beings.

38

RETIRING BRUNO AND MOVING ON

By early 1979 I was twenty seven years old, had completed ten years of service in the police and almost seven years in the Dog Unit. I had been a Flying Squad Duty Officer for eighteen months when the General on the Officer's Board comment about spending my career looking up the dog's bum seemed to becoming a reality.

Bruno had been stabbed twice, and whilst still very keen was slowing down a bit. He had done everything I had asked of him and more. He had been living at home with me for nine months so whilst being a police dog he was becoming a family pet as well. We had won the Eric Gordon trophy twice, and my role as Duty Officer required me to manage and mentor rather than be first at the scene of the crime. I was not interested in getting another dog as that would be a long term commitment, and I would always be making unfavourable comparisons with Bruno. I did not want to continue as Duty Officer just to keep a dog. We had both reached the stage where we should move on.

I was asked by a senior officer if I was ready to take a police Station Commander post. I said that I was and would like to retire Bruno. I got the vet to examine Bruno and agree that he should be retired as one of his stab wounds some seven months earlier was deep in his back leg muscle near his hip which made jumping over walls difficult. Bruno could now be disposed of as "redundant government equipment". The paper work went through and I paid five rand for him with an extra twenty cents added on for the newly introduced General Sales Tax. Bruno easily made the transition from police dog to family pet, although he probably did miss spending time driving around in the car with me.

The District Commissioner made a few changes to officer assignments and I was posted to Umbilo Police Station as Station Commander, where I started my career as a Student Constable when I was straight out of school, in short pants. I had no problems fitting in with Sergeants and Senior Constables who knew me as a student as I was used to command and was comfortable making difficult and sometime unpopular decisions if required. I quickly got into the office hours routine with occasional late night and weekend visits. I realised that shift work gave me lots of quality time off during the middle of the week.

I had been at Umbilo for about two months when I was called to a meeting with the Divisional Commissioner, Brigadier Gert Kruger. Two other officers were present. The Brigadier outlined that Kwa Mashu Police Station had performance and discipline problems and he had decided to send Lieutenant Wouter van Der Merwe from Somtseu Road Station to Kwa Mashu. I was to take over at Somtseu Road and another officer would take over at Umbilo. All changes were to be with immediate effect.

Somtseu Road Station had the smallest area in the district, with Old Fort Road as the southern boundary, the Umgeni River as the northern boundary, Umgeni Road in the West and the sea in the East. Whilst the area was small, it covered a part of the beachfront with high rise flats, upmarket hotels, places of entertainment, and the Kingsmead Soccer Stadium. The large Magistrates' Courts were behind the station and I found that I was responsible for the payroll of the police staff assigned there. Dog Unit colleagues would drop in at the station from time to time and when I read through the Occurrence book and Crime registers I could see when they had been active in my area.

The Divisional Murder and Robbery Squad were based at the police station and many of their hard core suspects would be held in the three cells. That gave me two concerns; the first and most obvious was that the policemen had to be aware that the prisoners would try to escape and would have no concerns in using extreme violence in doing so. Some of the most extreme prisoners would have the death sentence imposed on them. I impressed on the staff that they had to be alert every time they went to the cells. The second issue was that I did not wish to have to investigate allegations of rough handling of prisoners by the detectives. I knew the Commander through previous cases, and I offered all my support to him and his unit and told him that I would personally inspect the cells first thing every morning to enquire after the wellbeing of the prisoners.

The local North Beach Residents' Association was very active, and crime and safety was a key area of interest for them. The local Councillor, a pharmacist, Henry Klotz, who later became Mayor of Durban, invited me to speak at ratepayer meetings. I had to apply my public presentation skills that I had learnt on Officer Course and I needed an in depth knowledge of crime incidents and trends to brief the residents as well as to inform them on what we were doing about it. I looked to strengthen and increase the Police Reservists capability to have them as the eyes and ears in the community.

I would come home after work to find Bruno waiting at the gate. He knew what time I was expected and he seemed to recognise the sound of my car. It must have been strange for him to see me in uniform and not go off to work with me. I would get changed and take Bruno for a walk up to a nearby school field and get him to run after a ball to keep fit. His job had changed as had mine. Bruno became the family pet and protector of my family especially when I was away.

In September 1979 I received a phone call to report to Pretoria for a special assignment of about four months. This was the standard Counter Insurgency deployment, but it had a special require-ment. I was chosen because I was English speaking. I was instructed to take civilian clothing with no South African Police uniform or camouflage, or any form of identification or passport. I suspected that I was going to Rhodesia as discussions between the new Government of Zimbabwe Rhodesia and the two liberation movements had recently commenced at Lancaster House in London under the auspices of the British Government, as the former colonial power.

I was seconded to the British South Africa Police (the Rhode-sian Police) on a deployment that lasted six months involving counterinsurgency operations and election planning and imple-mentation. In March 1980, I was at a Police base in Mount Darwin near the Mozambique border when I received a phone call that the election results were to be announced the following day and that Mugabe had won the elections. I was to leave immediately. It had been a hard physical and emotional time living on my nerves as I mixed with policemen and farmers anxious about their future, Commonwealth Election Monitors, British and Australian Army Officers and a ZANLA Commander. In the last few weeks I had travelled to all the outlying police camps and collected all the informer reports and sensitive files and burnt them when I got the order to leave.

After a brief period of leave back home I was appointed as the Police Recruitment Officer at Divisional Headquarters. This was an interesting challenge and an opportunity to learn new skills at the seat of police authority, but I felt unsettled.

I was surprised that some of my friends and work colleagues were rather dismissive of the events in Zimbabwe-Rhodesia. It was as though they did not like the outcome and therefore put it out of their minds. Some did not think that this was a portent of things to come for South Africa; or that the African Nationalist movements, spurred on by international communism, would be encouraged and step up their activities. The establishment of African Nation-alist-Communist regimes in Angola and Mozambique and now Rhodesia would place pressure on the South African government to either attempt to crush or accommodate African aspirations for a better life and an increasing role in politics.

As a result of my experiences I came to the conclusion that South Africa would be forced to crossroads to make a crucial decision about African majority rule in around ten years. Economic and political pressure from the international world, and internal sabotage, coupled with politicising of the African population would impact on the future safety and prosperity of my family.

I had identified the long term challenge and I had to formulate a response. I decided then that I wanted to leave the police to get a job in commerce, and study to get some credible qualification which I could use anywhere in the world. I decided that my best option would be to look for a job as a Security Officer with a large organisation where I could observe and participate in a business environment. I could then identify a good course of study and hope to move into a commercial profession.

Three or four months after returning from Rhodesia, I noticed that I had been awarded the Police Medal for Faithful Service which was pretty standard for policemen who completed ten years of service with a clean record. I was also awarded the Police Medal for Combating Terrorism with a bar for my double tour of duty up North. I thereafter wore the two ribbons on my tunic, and received the medals a month or so later.

As the Recruitment Officer, I was required to hold exit interviews with all White policemen who resigned. In most instances, the men quoted insufficient money and stress as the reason for leaving. Some of the leavers were just worn out dealing with crime and violence and their families were pushing them to leave. They took a variety of unrelated jobs and this eased my fear of leaving. If they could find a job with at least the same level of pay, so could I. I asked the men at these interviews to speak freely, which they did. I saw their issues mirrored in my own; poor money, stress and an impact on their domestic relations weighed against a sense of duty, commitment to a team, and a feeling of service to the community. I thanked the men for their service and told them that if they wanted to consider returning at any time, they could do so as I would endorse their file accordingly. I knew that once they submitted their resignations, they were usually snubbed by their Commanders and colleagues. The police was a very close knit subculture, and leaving was to break ranks and abandon the group.

I applied for a job as a Security Manager in the newly established City Council Security Section and was offered the position. I accepted, knowing that it was going to be a major wrench from the only life I had known since leaving school. The transition was made easier because the Chief Security Officer was a former Police Officer colleague, whilst three former Dog Handlers had also joined as Security Officers and would report to me.

I wrote out my resignation which I took to Colonel Gert Schmidt, the Divisional Commissioner's Staff Officer. I briefly told him of my circumstances, and he was fine with it. A day later I asked Colonel Schmidt if the Brigadier wanted to see me, but he declined and ignored me as I had expected. Colonel Schmidt said the Brigadier had only wondered why I chose a Monday for my last day in service. I replied that I had some important meetings and I wanted to leave things in a tidy state. I brought in my camouflage kit, weapon and other state owned items. I chose to keep my Officer's sabre and was surcharged in the region of ten rand (R10) or the equivalent of five pounds (£5) at that time. They checked a list and enquired where two pairs of bush course socks were that I was issued with ten years earlier. I had forgotten about them, so they cost me around thirty cents. I had the last laugh though, as those socks were really tough and survive to the present day, almost fifty years after issue.

On Monday 9 February 1981, I walked out of Police Headquarters after twelve years of service. A few of the junior headquarters staff popped in to say goodbye but I was ignored by most others. I hung my uniform up in the cupboard as I was to remain on the inactive Police Reserve, but I never wore it again. This was the end of an era. I looked back fondly on my years in the squad cars, the close friendships I made and what it taught me. Relationships and friendships made under adversity, and danger, where our lives depended daily upon one another, are like no other. I had gone from being a well-mannered schoolboy to a confident and worldly-wise leader of a team, with honed observation skills and a deep understanding of people. I acquired professional and life skills and had much to be thankful for by being a member of an elite unit, but I had evolved as the world around me changed, and it was time to move on with confidence. A whole new world of challenges waited for me in a new career in the Durban Corporation Security Section.

Bruno remained my physical link to my unforgettable time in the Dog Unit. He was the protector and friend to my wife and son and he had a happy retirement. Father Time began to slow him down, and by 1984 he became a little unsteady on his feet and went off his food. He lay on his bed on the porch outside the lounge door and did not move or eat for two days. I tried to hand feed him raw liver and he nibbled on a little. It seemed he was doing it just to please me. I gave him some aspirin to ease his joints but there was little if no improvement. I took him to Amos and Clow, the vet who treated the police dogs and who knew him from his various consultations over the years.

The vet examined him and I asked him if it was the end of the road for him. The vet felt that whilst he was nearing his end, there was a little way to go yet. He gave Bruno a vitamin injection and told me that I should continue to watch him. He said that Bruno and I would both know when the time had come. Bruno seemed a little livelier and ate sparingly but he was very thin. About a month later Bruno again just lay on his bed and would not eat or move. I sat with him and talked to him about all the great things we did together; how much I appreciated his unconditional love, and told him that he would always be my special companion. Bruno looked at me with his big brown eyes as if to say, "I am finished. Please help me out boss."

I phoned the vet and took him into the surgery. I took my son with me to say goodbye to Bruno. The vet examined him and we agreed to put him down. I held him as the doctor injected him and I felt him take his last breath. He was at peace. Tears ran down my cheeks but I had one last duty to do for Bruno. I carried him to my car and drove him to the Cato Manor SPCA which was situated just behind the Dog Unit offices and kennels. The SPCA would cremate Bruno and store his ashes in an urn on a plinth at Heroes' Rest, the Dog Unit memorial, together with all his fellow police dogs including Flip Sonnekus's dog Rex, Fred Pautz's dog Caro, and Manie Odendaal's dog Prince; heroes all.

Looking back after many years, I still feel blessed to have had such an amazing companion. We shared dangers together and got hurt together. We fought the good fight, we finished the course and we kept the faith.

The inscription on the urn containing Bruno's ashes at the Cato Manor Heroes' Rest Memorial.

ABOUT THE AUTHOR

S id Brettell

Sid Brettell chose to do his National Service in the South African Police starting in December 1968 after completing his school Matric. He resigned from the Police in 1981 having been promoted through the ranks to Lieutenant whilst serving in the Dog Unit, as Duty Officer in the Flying Squad, Station Commander and Divisional Recruitment Officer. He was appointed as Security Manager in the Durban City Council and subsequently the City Chief Security Officer in 1989 before being appointed as Human Resources Director to several Municipal Departments. He resigned from the Council in 2001 and moved to London where he took up a role as a Human Resources Director for Europe, the Middle East and Africa with a Multi-national company contracting to Government departments supporting the British Military and NATO in the Middle East and other UK based Government departments. He retired in 2018.

Printed in Germany
by Amazon Distribution
GmbH, Leipzig

16083540R00154